Here's to

Making Waves

in Retirement

FROM WAYPOINT TO WAYPOINT

Cheers & Blessings!

Alfie Tounjian, CFP®

Alfie

Advantage Retirement Group

FORT MYERS, FLORIDA

Alfie Tounjian/Advantage Retirement Group
8870 Daniels Pkwy
Fort Myers, FL 33912
www.advantageretirementgroup.com

Book layout ©2013 BookDesignTemplates.com

Making Waves in Retirement/ Alfie Tounjian. — 2nd ed.
ISBN 9798795203850

Contents ✦

Alfie and Tommie Tounjian

A three-tier fountain once stood in the courtyard near the entrance of Advantage Retirement Group. When the fixture unexpectedly burst a pipe, an attempted repair caused the massive structure to dislodge from the base, crash to the ground, and reduce everything to rubble.

Several days later, while my wife Tommie and I were praying, I said, "God, protect those who selflessly serve our community and country and help us to be a Beacon Of Light." At that very moment, I had an epiphany. "That's it!! We don't need another fountain. Instead, we will erect a flagpole and call it a 'Beacon Of Light.'"

Soon we rebuilt our outdoor centerpiece where we proudly display the American flag. To commemorate the unveiling, we invited military personnel and veterans, first responders, civic leaders, and many others that we've come to know as our family of clients to join us for an event we called "A Beacon of Light." Our celebration included color guards, prayer, "TAPS," and ended with all who have served our great country, united together underneath the "Beacon of Light" as we listened to the lyrics of "I'm Proud to be an American."

The American flag now flies for all to see, both day and night. In recognition of the ideals and freedoms we cherish as U.S. citizens, I dedicate this book to our brave men and women in the Armed Forces and the first responders who courageously protect and preserve the country I so dearly love.

— Alfie Tounjian

Foreword
by Cody Foster

When Alfie Tounjian told Advisors Excel about the success and vitality of his financial planning practice, the representative handling that phone call for our company might have gulped. Out loud.

More than fifteen years have passed since we had those initial conversations with the president of Advantage Retirement Group. He still laughs, though, whenever we discuss those early conversations designed to break the ice. Alfie has even told me he could hear the voice on the phone change when he took our first call.

Three college friends, myself included, started Advisors Excel with the vision of creating an organization that supported the best financial advisors in the country, putting them in a better position to help their clients enjoy retirement. Every day I work with hundreds of independent financial advisors across the country. I see the vital role they play in helping people like you enjoy a successful retirement.

When it comes to success in your retirement, and frankly, your financial future, it's important to find someone you can trust, who believes in you, and who wants what is best for you. The author of this book, Alfie Tounjian, is that person. I know because he believed in me first.

After those initial conversations with Alfie, he continued to grow curious about our vision to develop a network of peers who freely exchanged ideas and allowed advisors who joined our company to help other advisors. Alfie had served in this capacity already after hiring and training a half-dozen other advisors. He was comfortable sharing best practices that made him so successful.

I don't know that what he divulged about his practice vaporized any of the sweat I felt on my palms during my first phone call with Alfie. However, the conversation instilled hope that a successful advisor might be willing to believe in some young kids trying to start and build their own business.

The favorable impression prompted Alfie to attend an IRA conference we scheduled for advisors to attend in Dallas. We charged $1,500 for the event, though we wondered if that price would seem fair to attendees while keeping our new firm from losing money we did not yet have.

Alfie laughed some years later when he said the $1,500 registration fee intrigued him. "I figured if it wasn't free, it must be pretty good stuff," he told me.

We still laugh too about a few of the speakers, but our time with Alfie in Dallas proved invaluable. My partner, AE co-founder David Callanan, ate breakfast, lunch, and dinner two days straight with Alfie. They always had Mexican food. Alfie has reminded us from time to time that he saw greatness in us during that event and at subsequent meetings, including one that convinced him to join Advisors Excel.

That's when two of us visited with Alfie at his home. Other financial partners attended the overnight gathering. We slept in bunk beds, but I remember being perfectly fine with those accommodations. For starters, being house guests of Alfie saved us money on lodging. Also, we didn't want to bring a big recruit like Alfie into our start-up since we were working out of the basement of a dentist's office. We worried, rightfully so, about first impressions.

Although I got peppered with questions by Alfie and his partners, my answers proved sufficient. The kindness he extended by opening his home to us launched a friendship I cherish with one of the most genuine people I know, Alfie Tounjian.

Today, Advisors Excel stages 60 or so events per year for the 800 financial professionals we represent as the nation's leading Independent Marketing Organization. Alfie embodies the gold standard we advocate in our industry—a pro's pro who is always trying to learn new strategies and improve on the value he can provide his clients.

Not only does Alfie believe in educating himself, but he believes in educating his clients. Whether through his workshops, on his radio or television shows, or through writing this book, he focuses on making sure his clients know the risks they'll face in retirement and how they can avoid them.

I know if I ever need anything, Alfie would be there for me and would do anything he could to help me. He's already done it once in a way he will never truly realize. I don't know about you, but that's the type of advisor and person I'd trust with my future. Come to think of it, in a way, I already did, beginning with thoughts that raced through my mind while sleeping in a bunk bed.

~ Cody Foster
Co-founder, Advisors Excel
Topeka, Kansas
September 2021

Preface

I saw a headline once that signaled an apparent high-water mark for an iconic generation of Americans. The declaration stopped me in my tracks: "**10,000 Boomers Are Retiring Each Day.**"

That's a lot of people!

And the tide has not receded. Those born between 1946 and 1964 represent the boomer generation. Based on that benchmark, the last of the boomers will turn sixty-five in 2029.

According to the demographers who keep track of such things, the "retirement stampede" began in 2010. That's the year 10,000 baby boomers began turning sixty-five every day. They refer to this as the "pig in the python" phenomenon. Because, when you look at a population timeline of the twentieth century, the bulge in the birth rate after World War II is a rather sizeable bump in what is otherwise a steady trending chart.

What caused this sudden growth in the birth rate is obvious, of course. Soldiers came home after World War II, got married, and started families. The country had also fought its way out of the Great Depression. With America's newfound prosperity, the more-is-better seemed to apply to everything, including the size of the family.

No other generation in history has changed the world culturally and economically quite as much as the "boom" generation. It's hard to believe that the generation that ushered in rock 'n' roll music, put a man on the moon, launched the hippie

1

movement, and coined the phrase, "Never trust anyone over thirty" is now becoming silver-haired retirees.

And guess what? They need to find a guide for retirement whom they can trust.

Is it possible to set sail on your own and live a do-it-yourself retirement? Sure. But I think of the many among us in southwest Florida who grew passionate about boating and wonder if relying strictly on one's instincts and impulses are the right way to go in retirement. Navigating the deep blue seas requires skills often gained from those with more experience. Even those who enjoy spending time on a smaller boat, canoe, or kayak as they explore the rivers, creeks, and back bays of our scenic Southwest Florida ecosystem likely developed their knowledge of those waters and the vessels that cover them from someone more seasoned.

Numerous threats can pose a danger for even the smallest of watercraft because conditions can always change, often on short notice. The bigger the body of water, the bigger the boat, the bigger the challenge.

Retirement presents such challenges. Many factors influence the creation of a retirement income plan designed to accommodate expenses you will incur, and just as importantly, could incur. For a retirement advisor, the formation of your income plan is like a sea captain devising a navigational plan. Much like the captain must account for any change in currents, waves, and wind, often with no visibility of land, a retirement planner must account for market volatility, health and long-term care expenses, taxes, and legacy preservation.

Working and investing with a trusted advisor can help you keep your retirement on course. I can help you devise a comprehensive plan and be able to make necessary corrections when needed. Such attention to detail helps keep your retirement voyage from straying off course. Look at it as if you would a boat in the deep sea. Just a one-degree change in trajectory could either steer you into the middle of a storm or lead to the discovery of a new island.

Baby boomers have redefined retirement. There was a time in America when you worked for the same employer for twenty-five to thirty years, received a gold watch, and started collecting a nice, fat pension. It's not that way anymore. Traditional pension plans are going the way of buffalo herds and polyester leisure suits. Only 4 percent of private sector workers in America can claim their only retirement account is a defined benefit pension plan that guarantees them a steady lifetime income upon retirement.[1] Pensions are more prevalent in the public sector, where some 6,000 systems exist in the U.S., according to data compiled by publicplansdata.org.[2]

For workers in the private sector, defined-*benefit* pension plans have largely been replaced with the invest-it-yourself defined-*contribution* plans. These days, you are fortunate if your employer matches a portion of what you contribute to these plans. The problem with 401(k)-type plans is they are usually based on the performance of the stock market. As anyone with a portfolio knows, the stock market has been on a roller coaster ride thus far in the twenty-first century. Wall Street watchers called the span from 2000 to 2010 the "lost decade." Why? Because, despite the frenetic activity of the market, when averaged out, the ups and downs resulted in little positive gain. Because retirement programs are no longer guaranteed, retirement security is a challenge for millions of Americans.

---

[1] CNN Money. 2021. "Ultimate guide to retirement: Just how common are defined benefit plans?"
https://money.cnn.com/retirement/guide/pensions_basics.moneymag/index7.htm

[2] publicplansdata.org. 2021. https://publicplansdata.org/quick-facts/national/

Retirees have faced other challenges the first two decades of this century. Some who were counting on the equity in their homes for support were hit hard when the housing bubble burst in 2007, and property values plummeted. Others found the steep decline in market returns that accompanied the start of the 2020 coronavirus pandemic to be difficult, especially those who grew impatient and began panic selling.

Look back at the start of 2020 and the waters seemed smooth as glass. The Dow Jones Industrial reached a record high of 29,551.42 on February 12.[3] Coupled with low unemployment and the economy had all the markings of another great year. The prospect of government shutdowns never crossed the minds of anyone. But later in February, a sharp decline began that saw the stock market lose 30 percent of its value in 22 days.[4]

To coin a boating term that is often applied to other disastrous situations, the economic fallout in early 2020 proved to be the perfect storm and affected many investors adversely. Just like we didn't know the storm was coming, we also don't know what the future holds. That sounds like a negative, but if so, turn it into a positive. By stress-testing your investments, along with looking at the fees you're paying and how all that plays into your income, a stress test for your portfolio can provide the insight to put you in a better position during retirement.

---

[3] Kimberly Amadeo. the balance. June 1, 2021. "How Does the 2020 Stock Market Crash Compare With Others?" https://www.thebalance.com/fundamentals-of-the-2020-market-crash-4799950

[4] Yun Li. CNBC. March 23, 2020. "This was the fastest 30% sell-off ever, exceeding the pace of declines during the Great Depression" https://www.cnbc.com/2020/03/23/this-was-the-fastest-30percent-stock-market-decline-ever.html

Unfortunately, as a class, baby boomers have been good at spending and delinquent at saving. Baby boomers, on average, have $152,000 saved for retirement, yet average spending for adults between sixty-five and seventy-four totals $48,885 a year. Do that math, and it's easy to see the potential income gap those averages portend.[5]

One of the challenges to retirement that wasn't there fifty to seventy-five years ago is that we are living longer these days. What's so bad about that? Nothing. That is, if you have enough money to last you your entire lifetime. But the concern we hear expressed most often from seniors is, what happens if I outlive my resources? Will I lose my independence? Will I become a burden to my family? It's a valid concern and one we will address in this book.

The Bottom Line

I want you, dear reader, to go into retirement *fully prepared* to meet these challenges. I would not want a family member or a close friend of mine entering retirement only to be ambushed by any of these challenges, so I do not wish it for you.

If you are retired, or if you are thinking about retiring in the next few years, and if you just don't have that warm and fuzzy feeling about the future that you feel you need, then you will find the contents of this book useful and reassuring. If you have a retirement plan, but just don't understand how it is working, you will be interested in what we will convey in the coming chapters.

When I first started hosting *"Saving the Investor,"* a financial TV and radio show that airs on several network channels in

---

[5] Barbara A. Friedberg. Investopedia. May 30, 2021. "Are We in a Baby Boomer Retirement Crisis?" https://www.investopedia.com/articles/personal-finance/032216/are-we-baby-boomer-retirement-crisis.asp

southwest Florida, I didn't realize just how concerned some retirees are about their financial future. For many of them, retirement is a new landscape with few guarantees and many challenges. When we talk about these important issues, even though I hold the CERTIFIED FINANCIAL PLANNER™ designation, I view my role as a navigator as much as an advisor. I enjoy educating people so they can make informed choices and prudent decisions. I love to see the light bulb of understanding click on when we can use plain talk to enable listeners and viewers to grasp some of the financial issues they find baffling. Nothing brings me greater satisfaction than to receive a phone call or a letter from a viewer who says, "Thanks for clearing that up, Alfie! Now I understand."

Establish Your Waypoints

I find that many soon-to-be retirees are, in fact, fundamentally prepared for retirement—they have the funds they'll need to establish lifetime income. That you've sat down to read this book indicates to me you're the sort who's worked hard to build wealth for retirement, and you've done what you can to start planning.

Still, retirement planning isn't a simple undertaking. During your working years, the prospect of retirement may loom over you like an unachievable goal. How do you go from a steady paycheck to thirty years or more living off your investments and savings? The key is to establish what I call, "retirement waypoints."

Many years ago, I discovered a love for boating. Some good friends of ours, John and Barbara, were experienced boaters and they proved to be a tremendous source of knowledge and instruction when my wife Tommie and I were just starting out.

John and Barbara had a beautiful boat that they docked up in Annapolis, Maryland, where they would often race it. Annapolis has a thriving boating community; besides the renowned Naval

Academy, Annapolis sits on the Chesapeake Bay, known for its beauty and agreeable winds and currents. It's a gorgeous body of water and, unsurprisingly, a frequent site for world-class racing events.

Just after I bought my first boat, John told me a story of a particular race in which he and Barbara had competed. In this day and age, every boat is equipped with loads of technology, he explained. An experienced navigator's insight is invaluable, but technology can often make the difference in a race.

"You see, in a boat race," John said, "there's obviously not a distinct course like at a track. To indicate you've followed the course of the race, you have to follow a sequence of markers."

In this particular race, a long stretch of open water separated the penultimate from the final marker, but the marker was clearly in view after turning the last corner.

"We weren't the first boat to turn that last corner," he said, "but I knew we'd win the race. I just knew we'd be the only ones to set a waypoint."

As soon as most boats fixed their sights on the final marker, they lined up for a straight shot and set the boats on autopilot. In so doing, they made a critical error: autopilot only fixes a heading; it does nothing to guarantee the boat arrives at your intended destination. It doesn't account for currents and wind—factors that can push a boat off the intended course.

John, on the other hand, found the approximate location of the marker on his GPS, and marked it as a waypoint. Then he set the boat's piloting system to reach that target. Regardless of sea conditions, John's boat did whatever it took to end at the waypoint he'd set. As it happened, wind and currents were especially heavy that day.

"You should've seen us," John said, laughing, "we practically looked like a crab, cruising along sideways to overcome the wind and sea."

In the end, he and Barbara won the race. Only too late did the other boats make corrections to get back on course, and it lost them their leads.

I tell this story to illustrate an important point: many retirees and soon-to-be retirees set their plans to autopilot. They think that's good enough. Set up the plan and just let it do its job, right?

Wrong!

Tragically, many retirees realize too late that they're not on course to hit their mark. By then, making the needed corrections to get back on track is either a grueling process, or impossible. Don't let that happen to you.

Instead, make sure your plan includes waypoints along the way. We call this type of planning holistic. It starts with digging deep into your true risk, something we'll discuss in detail later in the book. Then you must determine how you'll create income at different stages of retirement. From what sources should you draw income at any given time? How can you plan for and deflect market volatility? How do you adjust when unforeseen personal circumstances arise? What if your spouse dies, or if you die before your spouse—how can you plan for either eventuality? These questions and many more can be challenging to answer, but a good retirement plan will account for them all.

Much like steering a boat to its destination requires the captain to change course, if necessary, a retirement plan must also be flexible. It should accommodate unforeseen headwinds and not take on the kind of risk that can put you on a course that prevents a necessary correction.

I find that most of my listeners, viewers, and readers want the same thing: peace of mind and happiness. This book is written along the same lines as my TV and radio broadcasts. My objective is to simplify complex financial concepts and to separate fact from fiction. It is necessary that we understand the choices we make with our wealth, just like we understand the choices we make with our health. Can you imagine going to your doctor with a physical ailment, only to learn that he or she just wants to sell you pills, and is not really interested in your overall health? You expect a concerned physician to ask you lots of questions and learn about your health history in full detail before prescribing a treatment plan. It should be the same in the financial advisory profession, but unfortunately, this is not always the case.

In this book, we will discuss the difference between the "accumulation phase" of our financial lives and the "harvesting phase." When financial advisors don't know the difference and advise their older clients using the same investing strategies as they do their younger clients, it can be a recipe for financial disaster.

What you will not find in this book is a get-rich-quick scheme or a list of hot stock picks. This book is primarily about the money part of retirement, not what to do with the leisure time you have earned.

We may explore some new territory and examine some fresh approaches to investing. So, please keep an open mind, and hear me out when we come to those. While much of this book contains the same information as my first book, *Keeping You on the Retirement Fairway*, modifications have been made to update you on economic changes, the political climate, and developments stemming from the COVID-19 pandemic.

In addition, we are excited to add a chapter entitled "Women on Deck," which explores retirement issues women often must navigate. The retirement landscape is constantly changing. Keeping up with those changes is vital to financial success. *Making*

Waves in Retirement intends to help you identify different considerations you will face in retirement.

CHAPTER ONE

Finding Your True North

I believe in purpose-driven finance. What does that phrase mean, exactly? Simply that money and wealth mean nothing without a purpose. They are just numbers on an account ledger, or figures and digits on a computer screen, if you don't have a purpose attached to them.

I could go on for pages and pages here about how to acquire, invest and preserve wealth, but it matters not if, at the end of it all, there is no purpose attached to its acquisition and preservation. And everyone's purpose is different. I saw a bumper sticker the other day that bore the somewhat cynical expression about wealth, "Whoever dies with the most toys wins." I thought about that little slogan as I pulled by the car in the passing lane. If that was all the significance one attached to wealth, just the fun and amusement that it could buy, then, yes, I suppose it would make the whole endeavor pointless and futile. But that's not the case for people who attach purpose and meaning to their wealth.

It makes me think of a story I once read about a man who stopped to watch men who were working on a great stone wall, appearing to be the beginning of a church of some sort. He asked one of the masons, "What are you doing?"

"I'm laying stone," snapped the man. "What does it look like I'm doing?" The worker was obviously out of sorts and not happy with his job.

The observer moved down the line and asked another mason, this one with a cheerful expression on his face, what he was doing.

"I'm building a cathedral that will provide a place for families to worship for centuries," he said, beaming with pride.

The point is, if you have a financial purpose in life, your outlook will be healthier. Your purpose could be no more complicated than caring for your family. Just seeing to it that your spouse and children have a comfortable home and a good education could be purpose enough. You could have goals that include personal enrichment through travel. Altruistic endeavors, such as charitable contributions or public service, could be your aim. Or it could be that you wish to safeguard your personal security during retirement, and whatever is left over, you wish to leave to future generations as a legacy.

I had to smile at another bumper sticker I saw on the back of a motor home one day. It was partially covered with the tire of a trail bike someone had lashed to the stern of the road behemoth, so I had to crane my neck as I passed to make it out. It read: "We are spending our children's inheritance." I'm sure there was a story there and a reason why they saw fit to install that particular slogan on the bumper. At least you can't say they didn't have a goal!

Finding Your Purpose

To find your financial purpose, you have to decide what matters to you most. That may sound simple, but for some, it is like the $64,000 question. What do I *really* want to accomplish with my wealth? When you look past the basics of food, clothing, and shelter, what else is on the list? Security? Personal growth as a human being? Peace of mind? The truth is, only you can decide.

One person might think owning a home in the mountains and one at the beach is the ultimate goal, while another is satisfied with rather modest living quarters, but will not rest until they see their grandchildren successful in life. It depends on the individual.

But be assured that your purpose for money, once you establish it, is both your source of motivation and your rudder. It will guide you when it comes to investing, saving, making charitable donations, and especially spending, for the rest of your life.

An exercise I recommend is to get a pad and pencil and try to write out in one or two sentences what your financial purpose is. Sort of like corporations make mission statements. At least it will make you think. What DO I want to do in my financial life? While you are there, write out five distinct long-range goals. It is important to be specific here. And since we are dealing with money here, put a dollar sign to them when appropriate.

MY FINANCIAL PURPOSE

What are my values and passions? _____
_____
_____
_____
_____

What do I want to do in my financial life? _____
_____
_____
_____
_____

My financial purpose is: _____
_____
_____
_____
_____

My five long-range financial goals are:
1. _____
2. _____
3. _____
4. _____
5. _____

For example:

MY FINANCIAL PURPOSE: "To ensure that my children are sufficiently educated to begin their secular careers in life, and then to guarantee my spouse and I have a secure income stream that will allow us to remain independent for the rest of our lives and not become a burden on our loved ones. The remainder I will leave as a legacy to help my unborn grandchildren, with 10 percent for my church."

FIVE LONG-RANGE FINANCIAL GOALS

1. Create $100,000 annual income in retirement
2. Retire in four years
3. Pay cash for a new car in next twelve months
4. Pledge $1,000 to Orphans Hospital in next twelve months
5. Finish installing cedar sauna in old utility room by January

Those were just thrown out there as examples. Your goals will be unique to you because YOU are unique to you and your family. But the key is to be specific. Without specificity, goals are merely wishes. "Retire comfortably" is a wish. "Retire in four years with $100,000 guaranteed income" is meaningful. Why? Because it has the teeth of specificity.

Going over one young couple's goals, the wife blurted: "Make a million dollars!" when asked about their income goals. Then she laughed, and so did the husband. I chuckled, but thought to myself, "These are bright, young people–well educated and full of promise. They could do that if they believed it. But, because they didn't, it would likely never happen. They were selling themselves short, but they seemed to be very happy, which was worth more than the million dollars, in my estimation.

Remember, money is merely currency. It is an *instrument* to reach the real goal; it is not the *true* goal. People assume that we reach financial goals by investing and managing those investments. But the real path to goal achievement starts with your values, your passions, and your thought processes. A good financial "navigator" coaxes out those feelings and helps you identify them, thereby helping you create and identify goals. The next step is to put in place and quantify the objectives that are stepping stones to those goals.

Having $1 million is not a personal value, it is a quantifiable objective. The value is independence or security. The money helps us fulfill the value. It's the passion for the value that motivates and steers us.

> "Money isn't the most important thing in life, but it's reasonably close to oxygen on the 'gotta have it' scale."
> – Zig Ziglar

Money does not buy happiness, it's true. But it can provide us with choices and afford us the time and opportunity to fulfill our values. Like author and motivational speaker Zig Ziglar said, "Money isn't the most important thing in life, but it's reasonably close to oxygen on the 'gotta have it' scale."

Once you've determined your financial purpose, you have the goal in mind. Metaphorically, you've stepped into the boat and are setting your course for retirement. It's time to chart your destination, steady the wheel, and avoid the potential hazards that lurk in the deep blue sea.

Finding My Purpose of Money

Money was always tight when I was growing up. We never went hungry, and we always had a warm, dry place to sleep, but there was precious little extra to go around. Money – or should I say the lack of an abundant supply of it – was always a topic of conversation in our house.

It was perhaps because of this that I formed a goal early in my life. I was determined to earn a good income when I became an adult. I vowed to myself that when I eventually married and had a family of my own, I would provide well for them, and lack of money would not be a problem. Call it the exuberance of youth, but I knew beyond a shadow of a doubt that I could accomplish my goal. And, through hard work and perseverance, I did. Later in life, I would care well for my wife and family, and help provide a more comfortable life for my mother as well. My wife, Tommie, and I were able to provide a nice home and a good education for our son. So, financially, I did what I set out to do – or so I thought.

I was a church-goer as a youth. As young parents, Tommie and I regularly went to church. When we moved to Fort Myers, we started attending a new church where we liked the teaching we received there each week from "Pastor Matt." His messages challenged us to grow. One Sunday, the pastor was talking about tithing, the practice of donating a tenth of one's income to the church.

At first, I thought, "Oh, brother! Here we go again – another sermon on money." But as I sat there, something tugged at my heart and started making sense to me. I finally understood that what I thought was my money was really God's money, and that He had given it to me to use. I was merely a steward of it. I began to realize that my owning my own business was a blessing from God, and that I didn't earn it all by myself. God had equipped me with the ability to help other people, and the income that followed was merely a product of that gift. My thinking went deeper. "If all belongs to God, then why am I keeping it all to myself?"

When Pastor Matt challenged us with the idea of contributing 10 percent of our income to the church, I thought, "Wow! How could I possibly give up 10 percent?" We were in the habit of giving a little here and there, and maybe a little extra at Christmas, but I couldn't imagine giving 10 percent of what I made throughout the year. That was just over the top!

Tommie and I had a quiet drive home that day. We were both mulling over what the pastor had said. During lunch, we started talking about tithing, and it became a deep conversation. What was the purpose of our money, anyway? We decided to take Pastor Matt's challenge seriously and commit to tithing. In doing so, we found a new purpose for our money. It was not just to fatten our wallets, but to give back to God a portion of that with which he had already blessed us.

Later, I remember overhearing Tommie talking excitedly to one of our team members. "We want to make more so we can give more!"

What a pendulum shift! When I was young, I did not want to live an uncomfortable life. I also had a strong desire to build a successful business so I could care for my family and my mother. Those remain a priority, but now money means a great deal more to us.

When we realized that what we have is a gift from God, tithing and generosity became a way of life for us.

This discovery has extended into our business life as well. We now have a culture of generosity at our office. We are constantly looking for ways to bless other people, whether with a simple note of encouragement, or taking food to someone who is sick, or helping out in a ministry that provides food for the less fortunate people in our community.

I only tell you this story because it's true. At one time, I was worried that I would not have enough, and I didn't want to go without. Now, I feel so blessed that I have discovered the real purpose of money.

One of the first questions I ask people when I sit down with them is, "What is your purpose for money?" It is a question that only you can answer, and your answer will be unique to you.

Imagine you and I are boating together. You step onto the boat but do not see our destination. It is somewhere out of view, with only a body of water and waves in sight. What do you do? You trust me, your skipper, to chart the best course to arrive at our destination and tie up the boat to a relatively small cleat on a faraway dock. I have navigated this water and studied every potential obstacle. I want to keep you on course and out of trouble so you can realize your true purpose for your money.

CHAPTER TWO

Avoiding
Rough Waters

Working with someone who exclusively advises clients on investments could present some significant problems in retirement. Such advisors can serve you well during the accumulation period in which you are building a portfolio.

Yet, the expertise they offer and the concepts they devise for investment growth do not touch on every aspect of retirement planning. Their strategies can potentially jeopardize your savings if they incorporate too much risk into your investments or too much of your retirement portfolio is contingent on market returns.

If you think of a boat's draft (the minimum amount of water required to float the vessel without bottoming out), using an investment advisor to help with retirement planning can be like relying on the instructions of a boater with one foot of draft for his vessel. If your boat draws 24 inches, the advice you received may be inappropriate. The draft level within a well-constructed retirement plan should account for more variables than just growth in your investments.

Imagine heading into a rough storm that leaves everyone on the boat edgy and fearful about reaching their destination, especially when the rain and wind keep pounding relentlessly. Fortunately, an experienced captain can be a calming force. He projects a confident willingness to sail through perilous conditions, even when everyone on the boat appears distraught. Even when his crew begins to fear potential trouble, the captain provides a steady hand. His assuredness eventually provides a sense of peace for all his passengers.

An experienced financial advisor behaves much like a seasoned boat captain. He can respond to any sign of trouble, whether it might be a turbulent market, chaotic world affairs, or an unexpected pandemic. He has built safeguards into your retirement plan that help smooth troubled waters and protect your hard-earned assets.

I consider myself a *Financial Navigator*. My job is to help people who want to win the game of retirement, make the right choices and, *stay on course,* so to speak. I can't resist the boating metaphors, because retirement is like boating in many ways. You only get one shot at retirement, just like salty conditions may leave a boater one shot at reaching their destination on the high seas. And it is so easy to goof it up if you aren't careful.

My job as a financial "navigator" is to help you ride out the waves in retirement. What might those be?

Running Out of Income

The baby boomer generation is living longer than any other generation that has ever lived. That is a good thing *if* you have enough money to last throughout your retirement.

When I meet with people in our Fort Myers or Naples offices, I am often asked the question, "How much money will I need to retire?" That's a good question. No one knows exactly how long he or she is going to live on this earth. But I know plenty of people personally who are still going strong at age ninety-plus. They say sixty is the new forty, and there are lots of personal friends of mine who make me believe that is true!

More and more senior citizens are spending thirty years or longer in retirement. Having the financial means to fund that period in their lives is crucial. People shudder at the thought of getting to a certain age, and running out of personal resources, losing their independence, becoming a burden on their loved ones, or becoming a ward of the state. The real questions are: "Is there a way to keep my independence and self-determination as long as I am alive?" And, "Is there a way to use what I have now to guarantee an income to fund my financial future?" The answer to both of those is "maybe." Keep reading. We will get to that later on. But running out of money is one of those traps waiting for you, much like unexpected shallow waters or sudden wind gusts.

Getting Blindsided

As I sit here writing the second edition of this book, our country is in the throes of the greatest health and economic disaster of the last hundred years: the novel coronavirus pandemic.

If there's any lesson to be taken from what has become a global disaster, it's that things really can change overnight. One day, things are almost better than they've ever been. The stock market was soaring at all-time highs, breaking records left and right with no stop in sight. The country had its lowest unemployment rate in

60 years at 3.5 percent, and the lowest unemployment rates for African Americans, Asians, and Hispanics ever.

Then, in late March 2020, the world changed. The invisible enemy, COVID-19, rocked much of the globe. The United States government demanded America turn off the spigot that fueled our economy. We were instructed to stay home, distance ourselves from others, close "non-essential" businesses, and shutter our schools.

Restaurants closed. If they stayed open, it was for takeout only. Many will never open their doors again.

Forget about bad hair days; everyone had bad hair all the time with salons and barbershops closed.

We were told that hospitals exceeded capacity and needed thousands of ventilators for COVID-19 patients. We would have to build alternative hospitals.

I can't imagine the pressure our nation's leaders endured, especially President Trump. They were facing off with a situation no one had ever seen before. The stock market dropped 30 percent in twenty-two days, eclipsing the Great Depression's record of 30 percent in twenty-three days. I have been in the financial services industry for almost forty years and I have never experienced anything so devastating that happened so fast. I just remember praying for wisdom to keep my clients calm, reassuring them that we would get through this.

Coping with government regulations and red tape can seem like steering your boat through slow idle zones and creating no wake. The inability to progress can seem slow, tedious, and frustrating. Government activity can also impact the market and prompt many Americans to feel as if they are losing control and unable to live freely. Rather than live in constant fear, or worse, grow exceedingly impatient, it's essential to realize that, like everything in life, temporary idle zones do not have to be dreaded with uncertainty.

Partnering with an advisor who has experienced ups and downs of past years can help alleviate many worries about unpredictable markets to ease your concerns.

Several years ago in southwest Florida, the red tide and blue-green algae outbreak killed scores of marine life, destroyed local tourism, and almost led to looking for a different house that wasn't on the water. Tommie and I engaged in heart-to-heart discussions about our best move and eventually decided not to move at all. We had faith the situation would improve, and the setback would subside. Some of the same concerns, in fact, began to surface again in the spring of 2021 when several coastal beaches issued red tide alerts, and authorities cautioned boaters to avoid some of the popular freshwater boat launches.[6]

Although conditions can be miserable when the blue-green algae float above the waterline and dead fish emit a wretched smell of sewage, we stuck around before and will do so again.

The experience proved helpful when consoling clients during the COVID-19 pandemic, while also helping them strategically plan for their financial futures. If there was ever a time to commit to a holistic financial retirement plan, it was during this period, which would include a second wave caused by a new variant of the virus. But you probably are wondering, "how can you plan for something that no one has ever experienced?"

Warren Buffett, the famous "Oracle of Omaha," legendary founder of Berkshire Hathaway, and general finance guru, spoke

---

[6] Amy Bennett Williams. Fort Myers News-Press. May 24, 2021. "Is SWFL headed for a 'toxic vise'? Health department warns of harmful algae blooms throughout region" https://www.news-press.com/story/tech/science/environment/2021/05/24/red-tide-blue-green-algae-bloom-warnings-issued-southwest-florida/5243024001/

out to answer that very question. In brief, his answer was always plan for the worst. Buffett didn't know that our world would plunge into sickness exactly when and how it did, but he said in March 2020, "I've always felt a pandemic would happen sometime." How's that for planning for the worst?

The point is not to outline every conceivable disaster that could strike and guard against it. Instead, a holistic plan establishes general parameters for what could happen to our economy under any number of circumstances, and it aims to protect your assets accordingly. Failing to plan in this way can leave you blindsided when catastrophe strikes. Failing to plan at all, though, is even worse.

Imagine using the stars, the moon, the sun, and the horizon to calculate navigation. This technique, celestial navigation, is handy on the open seas where no landmarks exist. Not only do sailors employ such methods, so does NASA. During the age of the Apollo space program, astronauts and engineers relied on celestial navigation when charting their course to the moon and their return. The techniques used and a high degree of sophistication help night-time travelers adjust to darker conditions.

Today's economic climate happens to be cast in darkness too. The media tends to spread fear to drive ratings. It becomes important to sort out all the noise, determine fact from fiction, and gain clarity on precisely what political theater could impact our lives and our finances. I attempt to help clients gain a clear understanding of national and world events to help them adjust and make solid decisions regarding what could affect their retirement.

Failing to Plan

No one – at least no one I know of – consciously plans to fail. That would be contrary to logic and human nature, wouldn't it?

But the woods are full of people who fail to plan. It has even become proverbial: "People don't plan to fail – they just fail to plan." Why is that? For some, it is because they are intimidated by all the choices they have to make. Take Social Security decisions for example. Most people are eligible to take their Social Security at age sixty-two. But should they? Or, should they wait until age sixty-six, which is what the Social Security Administration calls the full retirement age for most Americans today? Or, should they postpone it until age seventy?

Decisions associated with planning can be intimidating. It's like the person who once got a job sorting bad oranges off a conveyer belt. Someone once asked him how he liked his job.

"It's OK except for the pressure," he responded.

"Pressure? What pressure? All you do is toss bad oranges off a conveyer belt!"

"I know," he said. "But all day long, it's nothing but decisions, decisions, decisions!"

We may feel that way without a guide, a "navigator" to help us. We will get to that, too. So just stay tuned.

Paralysis Through Analysis

Over-analyzing various financial elements can create some choppy waves that I like to help people avoid when they enter the retirement zone. This syndrome is the exact opposite of ignoring the problem. Unlike those who ignore the problem, the over-analyzers wind up thinking about it so much they can't make a decision. The expression for that is "paralysis through analysis." I believe that everybody will have between five and eight really great opportunities in life, but many fail to take advantage of them because they just aren't sure they have collected enough data.

Determining what data is pertinent can often be an issue best left to a trained financial professional. Consider again the priorities of a boater. First, they know they must rely on navigational tools such as a compass, depth tracker, radar, radio, and perhaps the moon and the stars to reach their desired destination.

If their livelihood depends on such navigational tools, once they shove off and are out to sea, some sailors are completely at peace with the world. Their quality of life is not affected by the ramblings of partisan gridlock, wild speculation regarding the future, or in the case of the 2020 financial downturn, even a global pandemic.

The COVID-19 outbreak initially devastated our economy — in particular, the tourism and service industries that are so essential in southwest Florida — and adversely affected millions of lives. However, many sailors remained afloat on various waterways. Their quality of life did not plunge at all because they never relied solely on the news of the day for information relevant to their lifestyles.

Filtering out nonessential noise, including the rants of fearmongering media, can be especially vital when it comes to investing.

During your working years, when most of the sand is in the top half of your hourglass, you are bolder with your investment decisions, and this is altogether appropriate. You are still in the accumulation phase of your financial life. Time is on your side. Once you retire and cut the umbilical paycheck cord, you are dealing with what essentially becomes a nonrenewable resource. So, playing it *safer* should be your watchword. But you can become so careful that you don't allow your money to work for you. In helping you avoid this tendency, my job as your financial navigator is to show you ways you can retire with confidence –

with the goal of knowing for certain that your assets are prudently allocated.

If you are an analyzer, you will need not hollow promises, but *proof* based on accurate information that your finances are properly positioned. You need to be comfortable with this knowledge, just the way you know your right shoe is on your right foot and your left shoe is on your left foot. Investing and preparing for retirement can be somewhat complex, but a good financial navigator should be able to take the mystery out of all of it for you. You may be surprised, as you continue reading, at how many strategies and financial tools are available to you these days if you are entering retirement.

A good financial navigator will also listen and observe with the goal of coordinating all counsel, advice, and recommendations to your unique financial situation and goals. A good ship captain will understand the water conditions prevalent each day. My job is to know and understand the environment in which you will be investing and saving for your retirement. The economy and the financial landscape are constantly changing. Changing with it is necessary if your portfolio is to thrive. A financial navigator helps you understand how the market works and the facts about investing, so their movements can be sure-footed, and they can be confident of the ground on which they are standing financially.

"Retire with confidence" is a recurring theme you will read in my firm's literature and on the company's website, http://savingtheinvestor.com. Confidence is an ethereal quality of the mind and heart. Confidence is an emotion, true, but not a baseless one. When it comes to investing, the foundation of confidence is understanding. I will help you understand how the market works, the facts about investing, and how to be a prudent investor.

Investing Emotionally

Here's a condition that trips up many a retiree – trying to time the stock market by looking for that next Google or Apple stock; landing the big one, as they say. Chapter 3 in this book will deal with this. Look for it later on, as we present scientific evidence that helps dispel the myth that it is possible to predict precisely what any market will do (and it *is* a myth, despite the insistence and repetitions of some financial advisors). We will discuss the emotions of investing and how to work around falling victim to them.

"But wait a minute, Alfie," I can hear someone out there say. "What about those mutual fund managers who have five-star ratings? Aren't they possessed with special knowledge beyond what is normal? Aren't they blessed with IQs so high they can just know which way the market will move before the opening bell?" Well – and I'm sorry to be the one to burst this bubble if you believe in this fairy tale, but – the short answer is no. They can't, they aren't, and they don't. But keep reading. We will get to that, and how the mutual fund rating system works, and what investors need to be on the lookout for in that regard.

DO-IT-YOURSELFER?

Are you a do-it-yourselfer? On some things, I am. And it has backfired on me occasionally. Recently, when a toilet began leaking at our house, my wife, Tommie, asked me to call a plumber. From somewhere deep within me, an urge to fix it myself came to the fore. "I can handle it," I said with a note of self-confidence. "Let me take a look."

The leak appeared to be coming from the tank above the toilet bowl. Determined to find its source, I sat on the toilet seat, facing the tank and started my investigation by removing the tank lid. I put the ceramic lid on my lap and asked Tommie to roll up my sleeves so I could put my hands into the water and feel around for whatever was loose. But everything seemed to be tight.

With my hands wet, I grasped the lid to put it back on the tank. This is where things went bad. The lid slipped out of my hands and came crashing down on top of the tank, cracking the ceramic. Now, water was rushing all over the floor. "Grab a bucket," I yelled, quickly flushing the toilet to slow the flood. I finally found the valve and turned off the water supply, and stood up to survey the damage.

Needless to say, we had to replace the whole toilet, and what was once a $100 plumber's repair job had now become a $600 lesson on why it is sometimes wise to leave it to the professionals.

Long-Term-Care Costs

The cost of long-term care is the "elephant in the room." Many people just don't want to talk about it, but it is there. There is a chance you will someday need home health care, assisted living, or nursing home care. It may be stating the obvious, but ignoring a threat is not a good way of dealing with it.

"Isn't that covered under Medicare?"

The short answer is no. Ordinary health insurance doesn't cover it either. And covering the cost of long-term care can rob you of a large portion of your life's savings.

Some people change the subject on this one because the only solution they know about is traditional long-term-care insurance, and they usually don't start thinking about purchasing it until it becomes prohibitively expensive. We will present some alternative solutions in this book you may find interesting. Of course, the best way to avoid this eventuality is to stay healthy, live a good, long life, and die with your boots on. However, according to statistics, the chances of needing some type of long-term health care are as follows: Someone turning age sixty-five today has almost a **70 percent** chance of needing some type of long-term-care services and support in their remaining years. Women typically need care longer (3.7 years) than men (2.2 years). One-third of today's sixty-five-year-olds may never need long-term care support, but **20 percent** will need it for longer than five years.[7]

So, we need to talk about the "elephant in the room" from a standpoint of what you can *feasibly* do to keep that ominous potential hazard from diminishing your nest egg and financially wrecking your retirement.

---

[7] LongTermCare.gov. February 18, 2020. "How Much Care Will You Need?" https://acl.gov/ltc/basic-needs/how-much-care-will-you-need

Sequence of Returns Risk

If you haven't heard of this one, we need to talk. It can be a monster. It can potentially eat up more retirement assets than the big fish that cannot be hooked on light tackle, especially for those who aren't paying attention to where their assets are positioned *when they enter retirement*. Particularly vulnerable to this pitfall are those who believe in exclusively following the "myth" of the so-called "4 percent rule" of investing. We will climb into that in more detail later, but this is one you need to avoid at all costs.

False Diversification

True diversification can be a good thing – a great thing. The problem is that some investors *think* they are diversified when they are not. We will get into what true diversification is and what it is not and how you can tell the difference. But let me give you the gist of it now.

People misinterpret diversity in a few ways. For one, they think different assets of the same class qualify as diversified. That's often the "diversification" a broker talks about. But think about it, just because your portfolio includes shares from fifty different stocks, will the variety prevent you from major loss if the stock market crashes? No. The stock market is down. In turn, each of your assets—with perhaps a few exceptions—has likely lost considerable value.

To help prevent such a thing from happening, a truly diversified portfolio allocates money to truly distinct investment types and asset classes. Often, a well-balanced portfolio will see some assets accrue value as others drop off—offering the opportunity for stabilization.

A second false diversification is the notion that fund managers do the work of diversifying for you. In a way, this is true. But ask yourself, do investment and financial services companies like Vanguard, Fidelity, and T-Rowe Price have the best fund managers in every category? Of course not. So, if you invest all your money with one of these companies, you can be pretty sure its managers will be really good at picking certain types of investments, and perhaps not so great at selecting others. This isn't meant to be a dig at large money management firms; it's just a reality of how corporations operate.

On the other hand, wouldn't it be amazing if you could hand pick fund managers for each category type? Well, that's exactly what we do. We use a rigorous process of elimination to weed through hundreds of fund managers and select those we partner with for our portfolios. We closely monitor fund managers after choosing them. If they fail to meet our standards, they are replaced. It sounds harsh, but I call it accountability. After all, this is your money we're talking about. There's no room for error; we need the best we can find.

In selecting fund managers, one question we ask every time is, "how much of your own money do you invest in the fund you manage?" It's important to me that managers have skin in the game. If fund managers aren't confident enough to invest their own money in the funds they manage, why should you trust them to make wise choices with your money? You shouldn't, in my opinion. You'd be surprised, however, to learn how often the answer to that question is, "no." That one question has eliminated over 1,500 potential managers. Some firms receive a kickback when they have their clients invest in a particular fund. This is called revenue sharing. Be careful not to do business with a firm that participates in this practice. If fund managers are getting paid to have their clients invest in something, do you think that they are going to spend as much time ensuring that this investment is really in their clients' best interest? Their intentions might be muddied. We make it a point that our managers do not participate in revenue sharing.

Bad Advice

There's only one thing worse than not having advice when heading out to sea, and that's having bad advice.

Numerous tourists, and some locals, choose to spend money on a fishing expedition while enjoying our Florida coastline. Success often depends on a crew's experience, instincts, and wisdom. They prepare by discovering the best locations for particular seasons, furnishing the best equipment, providing tips for what to do after hooking a prize catch, and never running out of bait. The best fishing charters excel at reading water conditions, feeding frenzies among fish, and the weather. They should also approach their clients and make them comfortable with the excursion.

The correct rig should enable everyone on board to catch an abundance of trophy fish after the crew searches to find the best spots rather than racing to the same location day after day along with other anglers. In time, fish move on, and an ambivalent crew will be left to provide a sheepish explanation, or perhaps even lie, to paying customers. That hardly qualifies as good advice.

We have a chapter on getting good financial advice and how you can determine if the advice you are following is the best for your individual situation. When it comes to financial planning and avoiding the choppy waves of retirement, no two individuals are alike. That is why there should be no cookie-cutter plans out there, but you would be surprised at how many people either have no plan or are following a financial strategy designed for the masses and not them as individuals.

I want you to remember the onset of the pandemic and the subsequent reaction for coping with the unknown presented by a new worldwide virus. Confusion reigned at times because of conflicting information we heard from medical professionals, government officials, and media outlets. Uncertainty spawned turbulence in the market. Leaders in each state, and even municipalities, interpreted shutdowns differently, with some places reopening long before others. Nothing seemed universal.

The fear created by the unknown, and the inability to fully recognize its dimensions caused many to be indecisive or simply freeze when considering financial decisions. We saw this in people who called our office looking for solutions. Many seemed afraid to make financial decisions because of the traumatic ordeal presented by the virus, including the steep downturn the pandemic initially triggered in the market. Despite Warren Buffett's contention that "you need to be greedy when everyone is fearful and fearful when everyone is greedy," it can be difficult during adverse times to make decisions for positioning your life savings.

But a remedy exists. First, have your plan stress-tested to determine how it will likely perform during good and bad times. Second, follow a plan to make sure it is producing income regardless of economic factors so you can gain confidence and comfort in getting through retirement. This remedy is at the core of what we offer our clients with the Retirement Simulator Process, which we will detail in the next chapter.

CHAPTER THREE

Planning for Eighty-Five and Beyond

Often it seems we take for granted the training that prepares commercial airline pilots to handle the many responsibilities entrusted to them.

Nonetheless, you don't just step into the cockpit and immediately command all the gauges and devices associated with flying a plane.

One of our dear friends flew as a pilot for American Airlines before retiring. He shared some of the training exercises pilots must complete every nine months to satisfy federal requirements and the standards set by the airline.

Pilots practice emergency procedures within the simulator, such as what to do if an engine fails, a bird strikes the plane, or the cabin experiences a loss of oxygen. Pilots also must complete training on aviation security and crew resource management procedures while maintaining technical proficiency.[8] Pilots also must follow the rules designed to prevent fatigue by imposing satisfactory rest periods.

I became fascinated by all the details included in the various training and re-training required of pilots.

Think about it. If a pilot casually mentioned before takeoff that the plane had a 75 percent chance of reaching its destination, you'd be pounding on the door to go back down the jetway and into the terminal. It is reassuring to know that airline pilots train extensively to be proficient at recognizing any potential dangers.

I am, grateful for all their training. It even got me to thinking. The concepts we build into our retirement process at Advantage Retirement Group work much like a simulator. We prepare clients for a multitude of retirement variables and considerations that could arise within five areas of retirement planning:

- Income planning
- Investment planning
- Tax planning
- Health care planning
- Legacy planning

This comprehensive planning fits into the Retirement Simulator Process, which performs functions you might expect from something with that name. The process simulates how things could turn out for an aspiring retiree.

As we get further into the chapter, we will identify characteristics inherent to each of the five pillars of retirement:

---

[8] flightdeckfriend.com. 2021. "What Training Do Pilots Have To Complete Every Year?" https://www.flightdeckfriend.com/ask-a-pilot/yearly-training-requirements-for-airline-pilots/

income planning, investment planning, tax planning, health care planning, and legacy planning.

Living How Much Longer?

Well, I have good news and I have bad news.

What's the good news?

People are living longer!

What's the bad news?

People are living longer!

I don't get it, Alfie! What could possibly be bad about living longer?

As I said before, nothing, if you are prepared for it financially.

The one thing many seniors fear the most – more than death, even – is running out of money. Is it a legitimate concern? Absolutely![9, 10]

If you make it to sixty-five, the Social Security Administration predicts you can expect to live to at least age eighty-four if you are of average health. That's for men. Women can tack on about two-and-one-half extra years. Keep in mind, those are *averages.* One out of every four sixty-five-year-olds today are expected to live past age ninety, SSA statistics tell us, and one out of ten could live past age ninety-five![11] The way life expectancy works, the longer you *have* lived, the longer you probably *will* live. Back in 1900, the

---

[9] Ethan Wolff-Mann. yahoo.com. October 16, 2019. "The Downside to Living Longer: Running Out of Money." https://www.yahoo.com/now/people-living-longer-lifespans-not-saving-enough-retirement-185822063.html

[10] FIAInsights.org. "Americans' Top Three Retirement Fears." https://fiainsights.org/retirement-fears/

[11] Social Security Administration. 2021. "Calculators: Life Expectancy." https://www.ssa.gov/planners/lifeexpectancy.html

average male life expectancy was only forty-six! When President Franklin D. Roosevelt signed the Social Security Act of 1935, life expectancy had gone up to sixty-three. So, what are the chances of you spending twenty, even thirty or more years in retirement? Pretty good, though Americans' life expectancy dropped to 77.3 years in 2020 following the onset of COVID-19 after life expectancy averaged 78.8 years in 2019.[12]

Staying Retired

The days of the pension are all but gone. If you have one, consider yourself lucky. But does that negate the need for a lifetime guaranteed income? Absolutely not. Because retirees may spend multiple decades in retirement, it is more crucial than ever that they have an income plan, knowing they will have enough money to last them through their retirements. Not just any income plan, but one that guarantees (not projects) an income stream for as long as they live. If they are a couple, then "as long as they *both* shall live."

And it should be in writing. In other words, the guarantee should be locked down and rock solid.

It is a shame for someone to work forty years, then retire, and ten years later have to go back to work again just to meet expenses. And yet, it sometimes happens to those who don't prepare well.

Don't get me wrong. If you **want** to work after you retire, that's your business. In fact, I know of many who have rewarding second careers doing what they love. No, what I'm talking about is being *forced* back into the workplace because you simply ran out of

---

[12] Rich Mendez. cnbc.com. July 21, 2021. "U.S. life expectancy dropped by 1.5 years in 2020, biggest drop since WWII." https://www.cnbc.com/2021/07/21/life-expectancy-in-the-us-declined-in-2020-especially-among-people-of-color-.html

resources and had to seek employment. As I say over and over on my radio and TV shows, that's no way to spend your golden years.

Bottom line, now that we are living longer, we have to be wiser with our investing and saving choices. Russ Wiles, financial writer for the *Arizona Republic*, put it best: "The affordability part of living longer will require people to become more disciplined, improve their financial literacy and embrace assets, from stock funds to annuities, with which they might not have high comfort or familiarity. In some cases, it also will involve an adjustment in attitudes and behaviors."

Stanford Center on Longevity board member Russell Hill says that young workers should save 15 percent of their income and many older individuals could benefit from "the lifelong income provided by annuities, as well as professional money management help."

Wiles continued: "If life spans lengthen, more people will want to enhance their knowledge of financial basics — the high costs of debt, the importance of stocks and other growth assets, the long-term impact of compounding and so on."

I totally agree.

Allocation, Allocation, Allocation

If you are buying a home for the purposes of resale or starting up a retail business, the key is location, location, location. The key to a portfolio's performance is allocation, allocation, allocation. Think of allocations as a football team. Instead of individual players running their own plays, the team is working together, giving them the best opportunity to win the game.

For example, I've been a Miami Dolphins football fan for my whole life, but I marveled as their division rivals, the New England

Patriots, dominated the NFL by winning six championships from 2001-18. Their quarterback, Tom Brady, masterfully executed the playbook and capitalized on the strengths of his teammates. Brady further enhanced his reputation and legacy by engineering the Tampa Bay Buccaneers to a Super Bowl championship in his first season after leaving the Patriots. A great quarterback ultimately provides his team and his franchise a better chance of winning games and championships.

The same goes for a portfolio. With a "team" of asset classes working together, a portfolio has a better opportunity for return with less risk.

Financial Phases

The two financial phases of life are:
- Accumulation
- Harvesting

Just as we go through physical stages in life, we advance through financial stages as well. When you are in your younger working years, you are in what I call the "accumulation" phase of your financial life. You are working, saving, investing, living life, maybe starting a family, buying homes and cars, and doing all the other things that go along with the American dream. Generally speaking, investors are more aggressive with their investing during the accumulation phase.

Have you ever heard of the Rule of 100? It is an investing rule of thumb. Take your age and subtract it from 100. That's the highest percentage of your investible assets you may want to consider having at risk. According to this "rule," the rest should be safe from market loss.

What does that suggest for someone in their thirties or forties? They should have most of their assets aggressively invested to accommodate opportunities for growth. Why might that be appropriate? Because time is on their side. They have time to wait for a stock market to (hopefully) recover after a correction. When you invest each month systematically, you are dollar-cost averaging – buying as values go up and down.[13]

When someone is approaching retirement, however, we feel they should be more cautious. You enter the harvesting phase of your financial life, when it is arguably more important for you to keep what you have than to take excessive risk to accumulate more.

I had the privilege to tour West Point Academy with forty-nine other business owners. We were invited to see and hear what West Point is all about. What I learned was life-changing. It has benefited both my company and my clients. In particular, that visit stressed the importance of providing clients approaching retirement, or just in retirement, an intelligible awareness of financial issues they could soon face. In doing so, Advantage Retirement Group could also prepare more stringently for what lies ahead.

Our speaker, Brigadier General Bernie Banks, explained that West Point always plans for the worst that could happen five years into the future. Whether a threat could encompass cyber-attacks, socialism, terrorism, biological warfare, or riots—West Point, and the army in general, work hard to foresee the worst that could befall our nation and plan accordingly. Then Brigadier General Banks applied his presentation to us.

"What could hurt your business five years from now?" he asked.

It was a simple question, but it launched a powerful exercise. In my firm's next team meeting, we set about identifying everything that could derail our clients' retirement within the next five years.

---

[13] Dollar cost averaging does not ensure a profit or guarantee against losses.

Earlier I mentioned Warren Buffett's prescient ability to plan for future events. I'm inclined to think that he probably follows a model very much like the one I learned at West Point. It's based on a similar philosophy that we, like Buffett and Berkshire Hathaway, have weathered the coronavirus pandemic without significant loss to our clients.

The West Point visit was significant. I adopted some helpful practices based on what I heard that day. But it wasn't a watershed moment. After forty years in business, I've known for a long time that complacency can breed failure. I believe you must do *three* things to successfully navigate retirement:

1) Stay ahead of situations in which you have control
2) Be prepared to deal with the unexpected
3) Make changes when needed

Obviously, the second is the more challenging. It's also the more important. So many factors come into play when planning for the future. That's why I implore you to find a financial professional in your area who can help. If you retire the right way, you're only going to do it once. That doesn't exactly afford you much experience with retirement planning. Professional advisors, however, have gone through the process hundreds of times—thousands if they've been around as long as me. A good advisor will get to know you well, to understand your goals and aspirations. With that knowledge, they'll constantly monitor your situation to help ensure you stay on track.

Remember the waypoints I talked about earlier? Setting those waypoints depends on your unique circumstances and the life you want in retirement. But how can you stay on course despite the potentially violent winds and powerful currents of economic fluctuation, inflation, health expenses, and more? What can serve as your piloting system?

A good advisor.

The harvesting phase comes when you are no longer receiving a paycheck and must depend completely on what you have accumulated and the interest you are able to obtain from those assets. To do that successfully can be a daunting task. Consider your assets a nonrenewable resource and don't subject them to unnecessary risk or the dangers of inexperience. You can't afford to waste your nest egg. Not if you want to make your money last as long as you do. Give some thought to finding a financial professional with whom you click. It's a decision you won't regret.

The Retirement Simulator Process

Factors cited above established the importance of creating a process that incorporated elements inherent to what we recognize as the five pillars of retirement.

Let's take a brief overview of just one of those pillars, investment planning. Yes, in retirement, many people must continue to invest, even though you have reached the harvesting phase and could be withdrawing some of your assets as part of a sound retirement income plan.

The Retirement Simulator Process helps expose uncommon or hard-to-find fees investors may have no idea they are paying. It will help show them their true returns versus what they thought they were getting. It will help determine levels of diversification and potentially show shortcomings to correct. Also, and perhaps most importantly, it will help us understand whether the investor may be taking undue risk for the returns they are posting.

What comes next is crucial. When investors are taking undue risk, we show them ways to reduce the risk and how it could even be possible to receive similar returns on investments, and in some cases maybe even increase those returns.

A Breakdown: The Retirement Simulator Process

Income Planning

The foundation of a solid retirement lies in the security of knowing it's funded by reliable and predictable income. We'll start with determining how much you need and then structure a customized plan designed to get you there.

Our goal is to create an income plan that allows you the freedom and fulfillment you've envisioned for your retirement. This includes a variety of possible tools, such as:

- Annuities
- Investments
- IRA/401(k) rollovers
- Income and expense analysis
- Social Security maximization
- Inflation plan
- Spousal plan
- Comprehensive institutional money management

Investment Planning

I believe that true independence is gained by growing your money through investments. But are your investments right for you? We'll analyze your portfolio to uncover potential vulnerabilities and devise a plan to help reduce risk in your investments. This typically includes:

- Assessing your risk tolerance
- Adjusting your portfolio to reduce fees
- Volatility control
- Evaluating ways to reduce risk while still working toward your goals
- Longevity protection

Tax Planning

Creating financial independence in retirement starts with protecting your assets. That protection doesn't just involve reducing risk; it also requires a strategy for potentially maximizing how much you pay in taxes. We'll look at the taxable nature of your current holdings, suggest ways to include tax-deferred or tax-free money in your financial plan, and build a tax-efficient distribution strategy to help maximize your retirement income.

Health Care Planning

How much will health care cost throughout your retirement? Rising costs and unexpected health issues can wreak havoc on your plan. We'll help you identify potential health care concerns and how to be financially prepared to cover them. Your health-care plan may include:

- Components of Medicare
- Long-term care
- Life insurance

Legacy Planning

Many of us hope to leave behind a legacy of generosity. We'll work with qualified professionals to create a plan designed to pass your hard-earned assets to your beneficiaries in a tax-efficient manner. Components of your legacy plan could include:

- Maximizing your estate and income tax planning opportunities
- Protecting any assets in trust and ensuring they are distributed to your beneficiaries probate-free

- Preventing your IRA and qualified accounts from becoming fully taxable to your beneficiaries upon your death

The Value of a Second Opinion

Before you finish this book, you will get the impression I love spending hours on my pleasure boat. Everything about getting the boat on the water, taking friends out for a cruise, or just enjoying some leisurely time with Tommie are wonderful occasions I treasure.

I also love to golf. Many who play a lot of golf over time experience back problems. The potential for such nagging injuries makes me marvel even more at the careers of icons such as Arnold Palmer and Jack Nicklaus. Neither of these legendary golfers struggled a great deal with injuries, a remarkable feat considering they not only excelled on tour but also put on countless exhibitions, many after becoming highly successful businessmen.

Because of my own back pain, I wondered what level of activity I could engage in and to what extent my ailment would redefine my quality of life. In other words, how fun could life be?

Back pain makes you question whether you can do practically anything. Walking, standing, and even sitting can all become unbearable. Sitting, you say? Yes, the back tightens up, making it incredibly difficult to move in a chair, let alone get up from one. It can be an agonizing distraction when communicating with clients, prospects, friends, and team members. I had to sit at workshops I conducted, making the presentation less effective because I found it challenging to engage with the good people in attendance.

Consequently, my back pain affected not only the leisure activities I enjoyed but also my work.

I visited with a doctor who mentioned the possibility of spinal fusion surgery to connect some misaligned vertebrae permanently. Fortunately, one of the country's leading orthopedic surgeons happened to become our client at this time as he retired from his incredibly successful practice. I mentioned my back issues, though the surgeon probably noticed me squirm and wince before I said anything.

It so happened that I had brought my MRI results to the office. The surgeon examined the imaging and concluded that if my doctor recommended a fusion, say no thanks and walk away. When I visited my doctor, he acknowledged the severity of my back ailment and detected cervical stenosis. Nonetheless, the doctor also offered the assessment I wanted to hear, "You don't have to have a fusion." I actually grew emotional.

Now, I'm enjoying all our boating excursions alongside Tommie. I play golf several times a week. And I'm fully mobile when visiting with clients, whether it's at a workshop, on television, or at the office.

One element worked in my favor while dealing with an ailing back.

I got a second opinion. This can be important for many of the decisions we face, including retirement planning. Many of our clients spent years working with an investment advisor. These professionals can provide satisfactory guidance as you build assets during the accumulation phase of your financial life.

However, as you approach retirement and are in retirement, different considerations can surface. Can an advisor who concentrates on investments best prepare you for situations related to tax matters, health care, income planning, and legacy decisions? Especially when you are no longer earning an income and a market downturn could jeopardize your life savings based on an inappropriate level of investment risk?

I know a second opinion about my back problems provided some emotional relief and a path to recovery without a worrisome fusion of vertebrae.

I also know a second opinion about your retirement considerations can be helpful, especially with an advisor like myself who specializes in retirement planning.

CHAPTER FOUR

Taking the Emotion Out of Investing

What's wonderful about my profession is I get to meet some remarkable people. Mike Zeigler, or "Ziggy" as we all call him, is one of those who absolutely amaze you. Know that special feeling when you meet someone for the first time and immediately realize you want that person to become a dear friend? That's Ziggy.

He gives his heart and soul to supporting our military. He has raised more than $10 million and counting by doing many functions throughout the year to benefit military families. Our military is our front line of defense. We need more Ziggys in the world to help support our men, women, and families who lost spouses, sons, and daughters in combat.

My introduction to Ziggy came through a business associate involved in raising money through charitable golf events. Ziggy is a PGA golf professional who specializes in long-drive competitions, so his golf exhibitions are untraditional but exciting to watch. After all, who wouldn't want to pound a drive 400-plus yards? Celebrities who partner with Ziggy to raise money are among a who's who from various backgrounds.

One event I had the pleasure of being involved in was contested at Tiburon Golf Club Naples in 2021. Many of our clients came out to watch. Celebrities included Christopher McDonald, the actor who played "Shooter McGavin" in the movie, *Happy Gilmore.* We all enjoyed listening to Chris reminisce about the movie, especially since the golf event happened to fall on the 25th anniversary of the *Happy Gilmore* movie release. We auctioned off several amazing prizes, one of which was a round of golf at Doral Country Club that included lunch with President Donald Trump. Most importantly, the event raised funds to help America's dedicated service members and their families.

Another treat that touched us all came from accounts shared by two additional celebrities, Captain Richard Phillips and Navy Seal team member Jimmy Lindell. I had the great opportunity to meet these two and listen to them recount the 2009 incident that became the script for the 2013 movie *Captain Phillips,* which starred Tom Hanks in the title role. The movie depicts the events that began when four pirates aboard a vessel in the Indian Ocean seized the Maersk Alabama, and the subsequent rescue effort conducted by the U.S. Navy and its marksmen who served for what was formerly called SEAL Team Six. Jimmy Lindell led the mission to rescue Captain Phillips while he was held captive in a lifeboat towed by the USS Bainbridge.

What struck me most about the personalities of both Captain Phillips and SEAL team member Lindell was the humility each showed while describing the events of that attack. Their accounts inspired those who attended the charity dinner to contribute roughly $339,000 to help military families. Incredibly, until that night, the two had not seen each other since the heroic rescue.

I cannot begin to put myself in Lindell's position, nor those of the Navy SEALs, who killed the three pirates aboard the lifeboat and brought Captain Phillips to safety. The response they initiated and the courage they exhibited are truly remarkable.

The ability to remain calm and keep their emotions in check certainly helped these men understand their predicaments and gain a favorable outcome in adverse conditions.

We can merely imagine the horror of clinging to a lifeboat in the middle of the ocean and being held at gunpoint.

However, we face times in our financial lives when we grow emotional about our investments whenever the market dips. This sinking feeling only worsens when we approach or are in retirement because our time to accumulate funds and overcome losses has given way to a distribution period in which our assets convert to income.

Many investors cannot train themselves to act as calmly or as decisively as a Navy SEAL while facing the threat of financial downfall.

Nor can we all be as bold and calculating as Jimmy Lindell analyzing the moves necessary to save the life of a merchant mariner.

As a financial professional, I try to be as forthright and compassionate as possible when helping people solve questions and address concerns navigating retirement. That is why our television show is entitled "Saving the Investor." I have a legal and ethical responsibility as a fiduciary to put the interests of our clients ahead of everything.

Experience, training, and knowledge of the financial services industry and the many facets of retirement planning are instrumental to the level of service Advantage Retirement Group strives to provide our clients. Our goal is to construct retirement plans that help you establish clarity and confidence in your financial future while helping to eliminate anxieties, fears, and tumult that arise from aimlessly attempting to predict the future and unlock the unknown.

How can emotions betray investors? An age-old axiom of investors is "buy low and sell high." That's logical (and profitable), of course, but it often seems to be the reverse of what happens. Why? Because emotions get in the way.

To illustrate the point, I love the chart below from Philo Capital, an Australian investment firm. It says it all.

Isn't that exactly what happens? We want to buy low and sell high, but our emotions get in the way and we do the exact opposite.

DALBAR Inc. is a research organization that specializes in studying and measuring the behavior of investors – why they make the decisions they do. Each year they produce a report entitled "DALBAR's Quantitative Analysis of Investor Behavior." And each year the report reveals the average investor that does their own managing earns far less than professional investors for the very reasons suggested by the illustration above – emotional involvement.

To get a broad view of how the market is performing, all you have to do is look at a market index. The S&P (Standard & Poor's) 500, for example, takes 500 of the nation's largest companies and tracks the performance of their shares on the market. If an investor were to park money in an index fund and leave it there, his or her gains would mirror the performance of that index.

DALBAR's findings indicate that investors fall into the trap of trying to beat the index, however, and "time the market." There are several reasons they don't succeed. One is because it is impossible to time the market. I always say, if you are trying to time the market, you have to be right TWICE! You have to know when to get in and when to get out and keep repeating it over and over – a very hard thing to do.

Another reason is because investors tend to lead with their emotions. Even if we could invest without emotion, the market itself is an emotional entity. It floats on the emotions of fellow investors. How much is a stock worth? Whatever investors are willing to pay for it. So, intrinsic value has little to do with it when investors feel they won't make a profit.

That anomaly is what allowed bubbles, such as the tech bubble of the 1990s and the housing bubble that burst in 2007 to exist. Inflated values.

So, to put it in a word, the yearly DALBAR studies all point to individual investor psychology as the main reason why they leave so much money on the table. How much money? That's an interesting question.

For a twenty-year period ending December 31, 2019, the average equity fund investor earned a market return of 4.25 percent compared to the 6.06 percent average for the S&P 500 Index.[14] Even when the market performs well, decisions can leave investors a bit shy of the S&P benchmark. A case in point happened in 2019, when the average equity fund investor fell 5.35 percent short of the S&P's whopping 31.49 percent return. This

---

[14] Dana Anspach. The Balance. May 27, 2021. "Why Average Investors Earn Below Average Market Returns" https://www.thebalance.com/why-average-investors-earn-below-average-market-returns-2388519

equates to a $5,936 difference for a buy and hold strategy tied to $100,000.[15]

Another factor that hampers the efforts of individual investors is the lack of capital. The term the media likes to use for this is "missing the rally." If you are using your life's savings to invest in the stock market, of course you will "miss the rally" when you start to see what you have worked your entire life to accumulate slip away! For individuals to compete with professionals, they must have discretionary funds with which to invest. In other words, money they can afford to lose. This would be money they don't need to meet expenses. Most Americans simply don't have that luxury.

So What's the Fix?

OK, Alfie. That's the problem, so what's the fix? That's where the Retirement Simulator Process comes in.

Once we employ this process, you can see into your portfolio and know where you stand in accordance with your own investment risk tolerance. If it's broken, and you are at risk, the good thing about looking at a portfolio is you can fix it! If it isn't broken, then don't fix it!

Yes, you're thinking, but how do I restrain my emotions when contemplating changes to my portfolio? The emotions that sometimes play into investment decisions can be nerve-racking and distracting, a point I stress quite often on our TV and radio shows. Sophisticated computer software can help resolve such conflict, however. We use a risk assessment program, which our money manager researched when searching for the best tools

---

[15] Dalbar, Inc. 2020. "QAIB Report: Quantitative Analysis of Investor Behavior." https://wealthwatchadvisors.com/wp-content/uploads/2020/03/QAIB_PremiumEdition2020_WWA.pdf

designed to help identify optional risk tolerance levels to assign individual investors.

The determination of a risk number helps condition clients for volatile swings in the market based on their tolerance for riding the ups and downs inherent to investments. This helps prepare you for downturns in the market.

I remember a doctor and his wife who came to us as new clients. I asked how the previous financial firm they worked with determined their risk tolerance and matched that to investments in their portfolio. The doctor revealed a rather unscientific approach. The previous advisor, the doctor said, asked the couple to pick a number between one and ten to assess the risk they wanted to take on. They told me they picked the number, seven. When I asked the meaning of the number seven, their response was to look at each other, smile, and shake their heads. They seemed perplexed by the question, while I felt just as perplexed as to why a financial professional would gauge risk so randomly.

We all got a laugh out of this, though it's not so funny when decisions like these can have a significant impact on your life's savings. That is why we believe wholeheartedly in the software program we use to determine an investor's tolerance for risk. The technology behind the risk determination model is fascinating and much more scientific than drawing a number out of thin air, which the previous advisor essentially asked the doctor and his wife to do.

The program starts with an amount of money you're thinking about investing, then inputs your birthday and the age you wish to retire.

Another bit of information the program asks is whether you are going to need a large amount of money soon, or if you're expecting an inheritance in the near future. After these variables are established, ensuing questions are particularly revealing. The first question, for example, asks for a dollar amount that would be devastating for you to lose over a six-month period. Some will actually respond that they don't want to lose one thin dime. Of course, if that's the cast, you should not invest in the market anyway. People typically relent and acknowledge that they are willing to lose some money in order for the potential to earn positive returns in the market.

Let's provide an example:

An investor starts with $1 million. They stipulate that they do not want to lose any more than 20 percent, or $200,000. Now come the advanced questions. The software projects two scenarios for you to consider, A or B. Possibility A always reflects a certainty, positive or negative. For this example, we'll position A to be a 10 percent gain over six months. Possibility B represents a 50-50 proposition. For this example, we'll position B as a possibility of losing 20 percent or gaining 150 percent. Consequently, A enables you to be up 10 percent in six months. B is undecided; you either lose 20 percent or gain 150 percent. For additional questions, different percentages are presented and respondents continue to answer questions based on their risk allowance.

A team of psychologists helped create the questions used in this exercise, including the certainty contained in the A box and the 50-50 propositions fielded in the B box. Based on the A versus B format used to gain responses, eight to fifteen questions are posed to help determine a risk level appropriate for the investor being tested. Often, we've found that based on the responses provided, an investor like the one above, who chose $200,000 as an acceptable six-month loss from a $1 million portfolio, will discover they would be more likely to tolerate a $100,000 loss.

This helps explain why some people shudder when confronted with a market downturn, especially if they invested in volatile accounts due to an incorrect risk assessment.

We consider this risk evaluation to be an important tool that helps dig a little deeper to determine a risk number suitable to your tolerance. Understanding your own unique risk number, and recognizing the amount of risk you find acceptable, can help reduce the emotional ups and downs associated with market corrections.

Asset Classes

I analyze hundreds of portfolios every year. Many people think they are diversified because they may own 20 to 30 companies' stocks. What I frequently find is that many people have companies in the same classification. Most of them tilt toward large companies, such as those that make up the S&P 500.

When you think about it, the Dow Jones is composed of only 30 companies, headlined by the likes of giants such as Apple, American Express, Boeing, and Caterpillar. Thirty may sound like a lot, but it's not when you compare it to the 500 companies in the S&P. But typically, if you're in that asset class, and the S&P goes down, your portfolio is going down as well. If the S&P goes up, so will your portfolio. What's the point? The best way to position yourself is to have different asset classes inside your portfolio.

Which ones are the best to have? We don't know what the best asset class is going to be year in and year out. One year it can be small cap stocks. The next it can be large caps. So, to build an effective portfolio, you need to have many asset classes, not just two.

The only way to tweak the knobs just right and keep them tweaked is by regular analysis and rebalancing. That's what we do. That's why people like myself are here.

These days, with so much volatility in the market, do-it-yourself investing makes about as much sense as do-it-yourself dentistry. You can, of course, do it yourself, but you run the risk of running off the rails. Also, you might ask yourself, if something were to happen to you, could your spouse continue doing what you are doing?

With a Vision, You Will Flourish

My great friend John J. Antonucci is not only a clear-thinking individual, he is also a pastor. A scripture he is fond of quoting is Proverbs 29:18: "Where there is no vision, the people perish." Only he puts it in the positive context, "Where there is a vision, people will flourish."

That's essentially what our broadcast is all about – providing a financial vision so investors won't have to work all their lives and end up with nothing. Education and information can be the bridge to entering retirement with a nest egg that will sufficiently sustain you and your family. Education and information can be the difference between pacing the floor worrying about the future and sleeping well at night, confident that the next morning will be another day you can enjoy in the sunshine of your golden years.

Once you realize that trying to time the market is an exercise in futility, and that investing is a long-term endeavor, you are able to make prudent choices. Proper asset allocation and rebalancing asset classes are two essential aspects of that strategy.

Recognizing your limits is imperative. I perform some routine maintenance on my boat, cleaning strainers and charging batteries once a month. But when it comes to changing the oil or replacing boat zincs, I'll call my mechanic, thank you.

When it comes to designing your own retirement plan or managing your portfolio, it's best to call a capable financial professional. Remember the emotions you feel when the market tumbles. Realize too that when those emotions prompt you to sell, you have to be right twice. You must pick the best time to sell equities and the best time to jump back in. Again, proper market timing relies on luck – even if you spend your retirement years looking at the internet all day in what will likely be a futile attempt to grasp market trends. And to that point, did you really work and save so hard for so many years just to spend your retirement locking your eyes on a computer? Get on a plane and see a new place, take your golf clubs with you, or hop on a boat

We recently had a client who, before we met him, felt compelled to spend his days, and often a good portion of his evenings, hunched over a computer screen, watching the stock market ticker, anxiously watching his holdings' share prices ebb and flow. When the market tanked in 2008, he followed the same pattern most independent investors follow in a correction – holding on for the rebound. He held on until 2011, and recovered most of what he lost. He was convinced that the bottom would drop out again in 2012, and he just couldn't stand the thoughts of losing what he had worked so hard to accumulate. So he liquidated his holdings and decided to sit on the sidelines. He was mistaken; 2012 produced strong returns in the market. But he remained on the sidelines and earned nothing.

He was not alone. Many investors behaved in a similar manner after the 2008 market crash. And when you ask why they felt that the market was in for another tumble, their reasons were usually based on something they had heard from a neighbor, a co-worker, a friend or relative. Or, they could have banked on something they heard from an "expert" on one of the dozens of financial cable channels back then. Those "experts" have only proliferated since then, while exploring additional media platforms such as podcasts, satellite radio, and streaming platforms.

Our friend, who had been influenced into making emotional decisions based on all the recommendations he heard, realized that all that chatter wasn't working for him. He is now a client.

Again, we live in an age of instant information disseminated by numerous sources using different media platforms. When I first began my career as a financial professional in the 1980s, we didn't have the internet. Americans got their news from magazines. By the time they read an article advising them to buy, sell, or hold, it was old news. Now, at the touch of a button, we have advice coming at us from every corner. Is it any wonder investors, especially those who are tip-toeing into retirement, are confused?

We encourage people to save and invest, not with knee-jerk reactions to errant and unsubstantiated advice, but with a plan in mind – a plan rooted in sound, effective methodology and strategy.

Questions?

As you can tell, I am both passionate and excited about investing. I find it intriguing and challenging. It is not necessarily the simplest of subject matter to discuss. I have conveyed things here as simply as I can, but if you have questions, I understand. And I would love to answer them personally for you. All you have to do is give our office a call and we will make sure you understand every little nuance of this part of keeping your retirement afloat and out of rough waters.

Allow me to close this chapter with a fishing story.

Prize money offered in some of the richest big-game tournaments can be quite rewarding, enough that professional fishermen often make up the majority of competitors. Yet in some of these showdowns, pride often rides on what gets paid out on side bets, or calcuttas. Winning a calcutta is often considered validation for an angler who may have finished among the top placers landing the biggest grouper or whatever sportfish the tournament promoted.

Validate means to get a second opinion as verification. Side bets that spring up both officially and unofficially among fishermen can sometimes sort truth from tall tales and affirm an angler's skill.

When was the last time you validated your financial plan? Is it as good as you thought it was? A second opinion may be necessary to see if your income will last throughout your retirement. There is nothing wrong with having your current advisor's plan validated to make sure you are not paying excessive fees. In the medical field, a second opinion is an accepted practice to make sure a diagnosis is correct. The same goes with your retirement. Has your total retirement plan been validated lately?

Products vs. Planning

The CERTIFIED FINANCIAL PLANNER™ Board of Standards airs what I think is a hilarious commercial, but one that makes a serious point. It's one of those hidden camera type of spots. The first thing you see is a glass wall with the very impressive sign announcing that this is the office of Miller & Koehler (completely fictitious).

"Let me talk to you about retirement," says a guy dressed in a perfectly tailored blue suit. He is talking to a couple we assume are husband and wife.

"The 401(k) is the soundest way to go," says blue suit. "Now let's talk asset allocation." You can tell he is just throwing terms out there that make him sound like he knows what he is talking about, but as we soon see, he doesn't have a clue.

Then, we are let on to the idea that this is a set up when he asks the couple, "Would you trust me as your financial advisor?"

The man and the woman he is speaking to look at each other and both agree that, yes, they would trust him as their financial advisor.

"You seem knowledgeable and professional," says the woman.

"Let's be clear here. I'm actually a DJ," says the man in the suit, clicking on a video which shows him in ultra-casual attire, long, braided hair, working at a turn table and dancing.

The unwitting participants are flabbergasted. They can't believe it. To drive the point home, blue suit gets up and dances to the beat while the video clip continues until the commercial ends.

The point is that anyone can hang out a shingle and claim to be a financial professional of some kind. That's why I suggest looking for those three letters adjacent to your financial advisor's name, indicating you are working with a CFP® professional.

What's behind those three little letters (four, if you count the registration symbol)? A lot:

Education – The CFP Board now requires extensive education in the following subjects before they will even consider certification.

- Professional conduct and regulation
- General financial planning principles
- Education planning
- Risk management and insurance planning
- Investment planning
- Tax planning
- Retirement savings and income planning
- Estate planning

Examination – Completing the coursework just makes you *eligible to register* for the CFP® Certification Exam. A two-day test is offered every quarter at various locations around the country. The test is four hours the first day, three hours the second day, followed by lunch, and then another three hours to round out the day. Those of us who have passed it can tell you the test is no walk in the park.

Experience – The CFP Board requires you to have at least three years of professional experience in the financial planning process before you can be certified. In other words, you must have at least completed an apprentice period. No greenhorns allowed.

Ethics – CFP® professionals agree to adhere to the high standards of ethics and practice outlined in the CFP Board's Standards of Professional Conduct. They must also acknowledge the board's right to enforce those rules through its "Disciplinary Rules and Procedures," *which require CFP® professionals to uphold the principles of integrity, objectivity, competence, fairness, and confidentiality.* Last, but not least, you must submit to and pass a thorough background check to find if you have had any industry regulatory actions against you.[16]

Anyone can go online these days and order business cards and call themselves just about anything they choose. But it reminds me of what Abraham Lincoln said one day when someone asked him how many legs a dog would have if you called the dog's tail a leg. Standing to his full 6'4" height, Lincoln scratched his bearded chin and replied studiously, "Only four. Calling the tail a leg doesn't make it one."

What is a Fiduciary?

Fiduciary – Now there's a word we don't use every day, but it is one you should know the meaning of if you are seeking or following financial advice. It comes from a Latin word meaning "truth." Some cousin words are "fidelity" and "confide." But in the financial advisory profession, it is the term for an individual who

---

[16] CFP Board. https://www.cfp.net/ethics/our-commitment/. Accessed November 15, 2021.

is legally obligated to put your financial interests ahead of their own, irrespective of commissions, fees, or other remuneration.

A fiduciary is legally bound to offer solutions that are in the clients' best interests. As independent financial advisors, it's important to know that we are able to offer our clients many different options because we are not obligated to push a particular fund or insurance product.

Purpose or Performance

Imagine you have retired to Florida from a land-locked state. You have vacationed in Florida before and had the experience to go on cruises, snorkeling expeditions, and fishing charters ... or just rented a vessel and operated the boat yourself. You have the resources to sock a considerable amount of money into a nice boat, or perhaps even a yacht.

Do you make an impulse purchase? Or do you comparison shop and gather input from those who are more seaworthy? Remember, much of your time on the water has been spent propelling around a familiar and usually calm reservoir.

As nice as those ocean watercraft look, and as eager as you are to set sail on bigger water, you're probably going to obtain ample information from experienced seaman. Particularly if you have the money at your disposal. You didn't acquire that kind of discretionary income by making knee-jerk financial decisions. The key behind finding the right watercraft is recognizing what you want it do and finding the right match.

Let's relate that scenario to financial products. Products are merely tools to get the job done. In our home, on a shelf in the garage, there sits a red toolbox I bought a few years ago. In that toolbox are some wrenches, a screwdriver or two, a hammer, pliers, fasteners, and some other odds and ends. I must confess, my skill level with these instruments is limited. Unless the problem is extremely simple and straightforward, I'm calling a professional. They know what they are doing. We both may have the same tools, but a professional plumber, for example, understands pipes. A professional electrician knows the wiring system of the house and will fix what is wrong without blowing up the block. I have learned the hard way not to try to do it myself. When I do, it ends up costing me more because I have messed it up even more than it was before I attempted to fix it.

When I sit down with people to help them iron out a financial plan, financial products, such as annuities, life insurance or structured funds are the farthest thing from my mind. Don't get me wrong; we may eventually use some of those products, but not until I know the tool fits the specific needs of the client. To me, it is a violation of all that is ethical, sensible, and professional to sell a product to someone without first ascertaining whether the product is what they need.

One Size Does NOT Fit All

What is the most important decision you can make if you want to go fishing? Knowing what species you want to fish for is a good start, including choosing between freshwater and saltwater species.

But where do you go to find your lunker? What will they bite on? When is their feeding frenzy? Where are they hiding?

You can rely on tips from friends, and perhaps even strangers online or off, but do you really want to set out for a day that potentially finds you fruitlessly casting a line? Do you treat everything you hear at the water cooler as if it is gospel?

Just a thought, though it's a concept often used in our fertile waters, not only by tourists but also by locals: Hire a guide. The best charters stay in business and attract customers by knowing the behavior of various fish species. They know best how to make your fishing trip ideal, whether you're fishing the mangroves, flats, or deep sea. Those who hook up with charters often enjoy telling their stories, showing their pictures, and in some instances, pointing to a wall at their trophy catch.

Others who settle on free advice get what they pay for.

Many aging investors make a similar mistake. As they near retirement, they look to friends, family, brokers, even the internet for retirement advice. What they often end up with is a brilliant plan designed for someone else. For the other person, it probably worked well, just like how a favorite fishing rig or technique or might work out for, oh, Roland Martin. Unfortunately, a good plan for someone else may not be a good plan for you at all.

There is no such thing as "one size fits all" in proper financial planning. The reason is obvious. Every individual is different. Different hopes, different dreams, different desires. Even if you had two individuals with whom everything else was identical, it would be this way, or at least it should, with their financial plan. Imagine if two individuals lived on the same street, were the same age, had the same size family, worked for the same employer, earned identical salaries, and had the same net worth as each other. Unless they had identical financial goals, they would require different financial plans, because they would have separate and distinct visions of what they wanted their wealth to do for them. Even identical twins, who share the same DNA, have separate and distinct fingerprints.

That well illustrates why one-size-fits-all financial plans don't fly. They must be tailor-made.

Learning To Relax

I would venture to guess that most people would rather be shown or taught how to do something rather than figuring out a new endeavor on their own. Even prideful, and we might possibly say stubborn, do-it-yourselfers probably learned from someone who showed them how to cast a bait net, address a golf ball, or plumb a sink. You can watch fishing shows, read golf instructionals, or examine the manual tucked into that box the sink came in. But some hands-on training best reinforces proper technique. At least it does for me. Even then, I leave any work on a sink to a professional plumber.

When I bought a pleasure boat and wanted to take it from Florida to Baltimore, where I lived at the time, I hired an experienced captain. I reasoned he would train me thoroughly while doing most everything on this new boat. I would spend my time observing him while content I already knew port (left) from starboard (right).

Well, when the captain boarded the boat he immediately informed me that he had the lines. That left me at the helm ... for a solid week, actually, since I hired the captain for that long. For ten to twelve hours each day, we would discuss the function of each button or gauge, and what we might do if a certain situation arose. After seven days I had been schooled on what to look for when docking, out in the water, and on the instruments.

There are instructors and then, there was this instructor. Captain Roy served as a nuclear submarine commander in the 1970s and '80s. His admiral, he told me, didn't always know the location of Captain Roy's sub during the days of the Cold War with what was then the Soviet Union. America's chief military concerns always focused then on the USSR and Roy's sub would be the one to hit that dreaded button if, God forbid, we ever had to make such a decision. Obviously, Roy could handle any situation on the water with a commanding presence, despite being somewhat small in terms of his physical stature.

The one situation I will never forget during our week-long exercise together came as a bad storm started to brew off the coast of Norfolk, Virginia. Captain Roy called ahead and said he'd be coming in and to save us a slip. They told us which slip to use and to ease in the boat bow first. Then Roy headed downstairs.

As I steered the boat into this marina, Navy ships, freighter ships and pleasure boats could be spotted and I felt overwhelmed. I had not developed complete confidence yet in docking the boat and began to panic somewhat as the wind picked up. I had difficulty backing the boat into the slip as it shifted and caromed off the bridge section of the dock. Suddenly, I could feel Roy's arms grabbing me from behind. "Relax, Alfie. Relax." That's all he said. He went back downstairs without telling me what to do, only to relax. What a lesson. I took a deep breath, started over and steered the boat right into the slip.

Sometimes it takes somebody or something to prevent you from making bad choices in rough times. Roy's simple, but poignant, advice helped me through a rough time steering a boat in wind and current.

This account certainly can be applied to the importance of financial planning. After we complete a comprehensive retirement plan for *you, times will arise when it seems like the wind and current pick up and a storm comes in. During those blustery times you need someone there by your side to tell you, "Relax." You need your confidence restored and at Advantage Retirement Group, we will be at your side ready to determine if we need to make adjustments to your plan. It could be too we don't need to make any changes; we already accounted for the turbulence you're sensing.*

CHAPTER SIX

Minimize Your Taxes

Taxes are an inextricable part of life. And in retirement, you don't want to settle for tax preparation but rather someone who is adept at tax planning.

No matter how much or how little we earn, the government will always take its cut. Now, I know you are a good citizen and you dutifully pay your taxes. After all, it's only by means of tax dollars that America funds many essential government functions. We need roads, bridges, schools, law enforcement, firefighters, a military – everything that keeps society running and the American people safe.

Most would agree that taxation in the United States is fair (sure, it's a hot topic in politics but still, relatively speaking, our taxes are reasonable). After all, demands for reasonable government taxation were among the first points of argument to instigate the American Revolution in the 1760s. Tax law has evolved over the centuries since the founding fathers won our independence, and it has contributed to the growth of the world's leading country.

Still, you'll probably agree, while we're willing to pay our fair share of taxes, we don't want to pay a cent more than what we owe!

There's an old joke in the finance world you've probably heard. It's terribly corny, but it makes a sound point. The joke goes like this:

"What's the difference between tax evasion and tax avoidance...?"

"...About ten to fifteen years."

A real knee slapper, right? Here's the point, though – tax evasion is a federal offense. Tax avoidance, however, is the perfectly legal practice of ensuring that we do not pay more in taxes than the government expects.

But you may be thinking, "I've used an accountant for years for exactly this reason – so that I don't pay more taxes than I need to." That's normally the first thing I hear when I mention tax planning to new clients. But here's the thing, a tax *preparer* is not a tax *planner*.

I'm not talking about someone who examines a year's worth of receipts, forms, and papers, whom you see sometime between January and April, and who sends off your tax return on your behalf. In fact, those steps are only a small part of the bigger picture. Tax *planning* takes a holistic approach to tax management. It involves more than an accountant does, and in turn, it yields much larger savings over time.

Tax planning is about plotting every financial move such that you keep the most money in your own pocket. For retirees, tax planning is especially important. In your working years, with regular income flowing, overpayment on taxes may sting, but it's not going to change your standard of living. But when it's your responsibility to generate income for several decades of retirement, every dollar counts.

Now, let me be clear, I do not pretend to be an accountant. I am not trying to undermine an accountant's value. My goal is to demonstrate that an accountant plays just one role in the process of tax avoidance.

Believe me, it is worth it to consult with a tax planning expert in addition to your accountant. Every penny that's saved in taxes is a penny we can put to work developing more retirement income. That's what it's all about.

It's not unusual to find new clients poised to pay more taxes in retirement than necessary. Many would never have known. Many don't realize that with a few adjustments in the structure and formatting of their retirement portfolios, they stand to save potentially thousands of dollars in annual taxes. After sitting down with several new clients, we often calculate that many of them could save significant amounts on their tax bill. Often, such savings can happen with just a few minor tweaks to their investment plans. Think what you could do with that residual income.

Here's the thing: each year, slight adjustments are made to our tax laws. Will you, John and Jane Q. Taxpayer, be able to identify these annual changes? In all likelihood, no. Modifications in tax law, and methods for paying as little as possible in taxes, are best left for a tax professional to address and apply to your situation.

I can't say for sure that you might be able to save, but I'm sure you can save some. These days, unique circumstances exist in the tax world that can have a profound effect on your retirement income.

A Unique Tax Climate

In the United States, tax law is something of a fickle proposition. It seems like every few years, the Internal Revenue Service comes out with a new and enlarged edition of its already overwhelming tax code. The most recent incarnation of the monstrous reference book is 74,608 pages long. For some perspective, that's longer than Leo Tolstoy's *War and Peace*, J.K. Rowling's entire Harry Potter series, and the King James Bible *combined*. And the tax code isn't just longer than the amalgam of those other books. Altogether, *War and Peace*, Harry Potter, and the Bible barely exceed half the IRS tax code's length. I bet you didn't realize there was so much to be written about taxes, huh?

The IRS itself admits the tax code is ridiculous. When the code was first published in 1913, it was only 400 pages long – a formidable read, but not unbearable. Since then, things have gotten totally out of hand. In 2008, the Taxpayer Advocate Service's Annual Report to Congress from the IRS stated, "the most serious problem facing taxpayers is the complexity of the Internal Revenue Code." That's a tactful way of saying the tax code is indecipherable for the average person. Despite its honesty, the IRS failed to address the problem it identified. Six years later, it added another 14,564 pages to the tax code. Whose idea was that? I guess taxpayers understanding the tax code isn't high on the list of IRS priorities.[17]

To simplify things, I'm going to make a bold statement: taxes may be lower *right now* than we'll ever see again in our lifetimes.

---

[17] Forbes, "Tax Code Hits Nearly 4 Million Words", January 10, 2013; The Washington Post, "Ted Cruz's claim that the IRS tax code has more words than the Bible", March 11, 2015; wordcounter.net; The Washington Examiner, Look at How Many Pages are in the Federal Tax Code", April 15, 2016; www.irs.gov/pub/tas/08_tas_arc_msp_1.pdf

Now, it's true, I can't absolutely guarantee the accuracy of that claim, but let me explain.

On January 1, 2018, President Donald Trump's tax reform plan went into effect. It's the single biggest change in tax law we've seen for more than thirty years, and it may be a gamechanger for people in and approaching retirement. Tax brackets and tax rates have been adjusted to our benefit. On top of that, the standard deduction for each bracket has substantially increased.

I've mentioned the term "tax deferred" in this book already. I'll address what that means in greater detail in this chapter, but the most important takeaway is that tax-deferred *does not* mean tax-free. Money in a tax-deferred account will at some point be taxed. It can be now or later, but invariably the federal government will get its cut.

For many years, financial advisors have preached deferment under the assumption that retirees will fall into lower tax brackets after leaving the workforce. Frankly, that assumption is unrealistic for many soon-to-be retirees. Taxes are likely to increase again on January 1, 2026, when Trump's signature legislation, the Tax Cuts and Jobs Act, expires. That means taxes to be paid on tax-deferred accounts could be higher in the future.

After taking office in 2021, President Joe Biden revealed several tax proposals. He favored retaining the highest individual tax rate of 39.6 percent from the 37 percent rate established by TCJA. Wages above $400,000 would be subject to a payroll tax, removing an exemption for wages above $142,800. Also, Biden proposed taxing capital gains at the ordinary income tax rate for those who earn more than $1 million a year and limiting itemized deductions for taxpayers earning more than $400,000.[18]

It takes an in-depth examination of personal circumstances to decide how best to plan for taxes. Current tax brackets will not impact everyone in the same way. But one thing is certain: as long as the Trump tax legislation is in effect, you would be well advised to plan for taxes *now* to ensure you don't miss out on immense potential savings.[19]

---

[18] Huagun Li, William McBride, Garrett Wilson. taxfoundation.org. June 16, 2021. "Details and Analysis of President Biden's FY 2022 Budget Proposals" https://taxfoundation.org/biden-budget-proposals/

[19] Amelia Josephson. smartasset.com. March 17, 2021. "Breaking Down How the Trump Tax Plan Affects You" https://smartasset.com/taxes/heres-how-the-trump-tax-plan-could-affect-you

TAX BRACKETS EFFECTIVE 2022		
Single Filers	**Married Filing Jointly**	**Tax Rate**
$0 – $10,275	$0 – $20,550	10%
$10,275 – $41,775	$20,550 – $83,550	12%
$41,775 – $89,075	$83,550 – $178,150	22%
$89,075 – $170,050	$178,150 – $340,100	24%
$170,050 – $215,950	$340,100 – $431,900	32%
$215,950 – $539,900	$431,900 – $647,850	35%
$539,900+	$647,850+	37%

TAX YEAR 2017 STANDARD DEDUCTIONS	
Single Filers	**Married Filing Jointly**
$6,350	$12,700

TAX YEAR 2022 (TRUMP PLAN) STANDARD DEDUCTIONS	
Single Filers	**Married Filing Jointly**
$12,950	$25,900

Capitalize on Today's Circumstances

In addition to the Trump tax cuts sunsetting, and subject to changes if the Biden administration gets its way, there's another reason why taxes are likely to go up in coming years.

As of this book's writing, the national debt had exceeded $30 trillion, and it's climbing as the federal government buckles under the unexpected strain of coronavirus pandemic relief measures. Just in case you really can't conceive a number that high, which is perfectly understandable, if $100 bills were stacked to equal $1 trillion, the vertical stockpile would stretch more than 600 miles high. Want to go on a shopping spree? If you spent $50 million every single day, it would take roughly 1,500 years before you'd spend $30 trillion. Anything in the trillions is confounding. It's more money than the individual person can reasonably fathom.

Where do you suppose the federal government will look to earn the money it needs to start paying off its tremendous pile of debt? You guessed it – taxes. If the federal government wanted to wipe out the national debt strictly with taxpayer money, it would take almost $100,000 from each citizen, including children.

My point in writing all this isn't to scare you. The government will never demand so much from each American, nor is national debt a problem the United States plans to resolve overnight. But it's reasonable to assume that taxes will increase in the future to address the country's mounting debt – all the more reason to capitalize on favorable circumstances while we have them.

So, what does this all mean for you? How can you prepare to lower your retirement taxes?

What's Your Tax Bracket?

Before making any tax avoidance maneuvers, you have to know your tax bracket. In theory, that's simple. The formula is income minus pre-tax or untaxed assets. In practice, it can be a bit more challenging than it sounds and you might consider using a professional to help you out.

After carefully evaluating your taxable income, determine how close you are to the next lower or higher tax bracket. Ideally, you will reorganize income funds to fall into a lower tax bracket. But at a minimum, you must be careful not to inadvertently push yourself into a higher tax bracket. This is especially important when planning to gift large sums of money and with Roth IRA conversions. We will get into the structure and benefits of a Roth IRA deeper into the book. In short, you contribute after-tax dollars into a Roth IRA. You gain tax-free growth on your contributions and earnings. You can withdraw funds from a Roth IRA after turning fifty-nine-and-one-half as long as the account has been open for five years.

With pretty strong confidence, I expect we will be paying more in taxes in the future. Granted, I could be wrong, but if you get asked to make your own prediction, which way would you lean?

My tax forecast stems from monitoring government spending and how it has escalated over time. Federal government spending, in fact, reached an all-time quarterly high of $3390.92 billion in the first quarter of 2021.[20] Taxes, in theory, help cover the cost of government spending. Are you willing to bet that Washington politicians will show more fiscal restraint in the future?

One of the core components of our Comprehensive Retirement Simulator Process strives to help you account for future taxes and examine methods for dealing with potential

---

[20] tradingeconomics.com. October 2021. "United States Government Spending" https://tradingeconomics.com/united-states/government-spending#:~:text=Government%20Spending%20in%20the%20United%20States%20averaged%202099.52%20USD%20Billion,the%20first%20quarter%20of%201950

increases. We use a tool called Holistiplan, which helps determine whether a Roth IRA conversion is a suitable alternative for our clients.

The Holistiplan software examines both your federal income tax rates and costs associated with Part B and Part D of a client's Medicare. By converting money from a traditional IRA or 401(k) into a Roth IRA when taxes are conceivably lower than they will be in the future, you can save on future tax bills in retirement. The conversion creates a taxable event because taxes are deferred in the case of a traditional IRA or 401(k) and must be paid at the time funds are converted, though no early withdrawal penalty exists.

Such conversions typically are not achieved in one year, but rather, spread over a handful of years until you reach the age of seventy-two, when you must begin taking required minimum distributions. Limits have been established to how much you can contribute annually to a Roth IRA. However, there is no limit to the amount you can convert to a Roth IRA from a traditional IRA or 401(k).

A full description of how your taxes will be affected by a Roth IRA conversion is included in the tax report the Holistiplan software calculates. An example of that tax report follows on the next page.

Tax Report

KEY FIGURES

Total income:	$206,348	Average rate:	15.4%
AGI:	$206,348	2020 safe harbor:	$35,067
Deductions:	$24,400	Tax exempt interest:	$0
Taxable income:	$181,944	Qualified/ordinary dividends:	$1,542/$1,952
Total tax:	$31,879	ST/LT capital gains:	$0/$250
Filing status:	Married filing jointly	Carryforward loss:	$0
Marginal rate:	24.0%	Credits claimed:	$10

MARGINAL TAX BRACKET INFORMATION

CLICK HERE TO HIDE THIS SECTION OF THE REPORT

The marginal tax rate for your ordinary income is as follows:

Marginal Rate	Ordinary Income Threshold	
10.8%	$0 to $19,400	
12.0%	$19,400 to $78,950	
22.0%	$78,950 to $168,400	You:
24.0%	$168,400 to $321,450	$179,890
32.0%	$321,450 to $408,200	
35.0%	$408,200 to $612,350	
37.0%	$612,350 and above	

MODIFIED ADJUSTED GROSS INCOME TIERS

CLICK HERE TO SHOW THIS SECTION OF THE REPORT

2021 MEDICARE PART B/D PREMIUMS

CLICK HERE TO HIDE THIS SECTION OF THE REPORT

Medicare Parts B and D premiums can be impacted by Modified Adjusted Gross Income (MAGI). Amounts below are in addition to the base premiums.

MAGI Threshold	Part B Premium Adjustment	Part D Premium Adjustment	
$0 to $176,000	$0	$0	
$176,000 to $222,000	$59	$12	
$222,000 to $276,000	$149	$32	You:
$276,000 to $330,000	$238	$51	$206,086

Hypothetical example shown for illustative purposes only

Whether you file single or jointly, the Holistiplan report incorporates several factors, including marginal and average tax rates. In the example above, the joint filers discovered their annual tax rate to be 15.4 percent. When we examine the report, I tell them to ask themselves if they think taxes could average more than 15.4 percent in the future and how a Roth conversion could at least reduce their future tax burden. The whole point to consider is whether it will be better to pay taxes on a Roth conversion or wait to pay them later once RMDs begin from tax-deferred accounts. I tell my clients that if they do not have enough money to pay the taxes owed on the conversion, the process might not be good for them. Also, it is not advantageous to use money from the converted funds to help cover the taxable event created by the conversion.

The 2020 market decline stemming from the coronavirus outbreak and its adverse effect on economic output proved an opportune time for Roth IRA conversions. The market rebounded quickly once the country began to reopen after the initial health-related shutdown.[21]

If you converted $100,000 at that time, you paid tax on that amount but withdrew the funds at a very low point in the market. Depending on how that $100,000 was invested, the market's fast rebound provided an opportunity for potentially quick and substantial growth of the converted funds. Best of all, the funds converted into a Roth IRA will not be subjected to future taxes as long as the investor abides by the five-year wait period on withdrawals.

The Holistiplan is one of the most important tools we employ and helps you plan for future tax events. Many of our clients recognized the potential advantages gained from capitalizing on the low tax-rate environment established by the tax reform set forth by President Trump in the Tax Cuts and Jobs Act of 2017.

We encourage clients who confer with Advantage Retirement Group about tax-related matters to consult additionally with a tax advisor.

Is a Lower Tax Bracket Realistic?

If you can organize your finances to fall into a lower tax bracket, that's great. But like I warned earlier, don't assume that

---

[21] Patti Domm. cnbc.com. December 31, 2020. "How the pandemic drove massive stock market gains, and what happens next" https://www.cnbc.com/2020/12/30/how-the-pandemic-drove-massive-stock-market-gains-and-what-happens-next.html

post-retirement you will automatically drop into a lower bracket. I know, after you quit working you won't be contributing to retirement funds anymore. You won't have work expenses. Transportation costs may decrease. You just must fall into a lower bracket, right? Not always. In fact, that kind of thinking has put many a retiree in a pickle.

Think of it this way: after retiring, do you really plan to sacrifice your lifestyle and standard of living? No way! So, will a few changes in expenditures be enough to lower your tax bracket? Chances are they will not. It normally takes a more concerted effort to rearrange financial affairs to change your tax status, if it's possible at all.

In reality, many retirees spend more money in the first several years of retirement than they did when they still worked. They go out to dinner more often, they vacation more regularly, they invest in hobbies they didn't have time for as working people. It's often said that for retirees, every day is Saturday. They're spending reflects as much.

Eventually that lifestyle tapers off as age sets in, but rarely do expenses decrease, in my experience. Instead, vacation and hobby money are redirected to cover health and long-term care costs. That's all fine for people who planned accordingly. It's the optimists who expected low (or even sometimes no) taxes in retirement who often find themselves struggling when the tax bills look more or less the same as they did in the past. Don't make the mistake of blindly assuming a lower tax bracket.

Revisiting 401(k)s and IRAs

We discussed 401(k)s and IRAs in our chapter on pensions, but they're important enough to warrant a brief recapitulation.

Almost everyone reading this book will have a 401(k), IRA, or an equivalent. Most variants of retirement accounts are tax-deferred. Like I mentioned earlier, that means you sock away the money for years without ever paying tax on it.

But the taxman cometh.

At seventy-two, if you have not already started drawing from your 401(k) or IRA, you will be forced to draw some money as per the government enforced required minimum distributions (RMDs). Those withdrawals fall under taxable income. If you neglect to take RMDs, the government will impose a penalty of 50 percent of any RMD money you ought to have withdrawn, and that's on top of your regular income tax. Even if you make no other plans for your 401(k)s and IRAs, please, *please* do not fail to withdraw your RMDs on time.

If, on the other hand, you have a Roth 401(k) or Roth IRA, you will not be required to withdraw at any age. That's because your taxes have already been paid. In light of today's tax environment, a Roth account is worth serious consideration. Unless you stand to fall into a tax bracket with much lower percentages – an assumption I strongly advise you to verify – it may be worth capitalizing on today's low tax rate. Bite the bullet and get the taxes out of the way while they're likely "cheaper".

Many have saved by converting their traditional retirement account funds to a Roth account while they are in a lower tax bracket or while their tax bracket has a lower taxable percentage. However, I don't advise making that conversion without the watchful eye of a financial professional. Poor execution of tax strategy can, at the very least, fail to save you money. At worst, you may end up overtaxed with less in retirement savings than you expected.

A View to the Long Game

Taxes aren't a fun subject. Most people avoid the topic until tax season rolls around when they're forced to file a return, and even then, they may pawn off the responsibility to a trusted accountant. If that sounds familiar, I don't blame you. Taxes can be grueling. Exhausting as it may seem, however, a proactive approach to tax planning can make a big difference in the funds available for your retirement goals. We often think of taxes from year to year, but it's wiser to consider a long-term strategy with a view to saving money over several coming decades.

You've probably heard stories of the world's wealthiest people saving incredible sums of money in taxes. Sometimes, underhanded business practices are involved. But, more often than not, it's just that the world's richest people know how to use tax rules to their advantage. They're skilled at organizing money such that only the minimum is taxed.

You can employ some of the same strategies. It may take some effort, but with the help of a financial professional, the process can be relatively painless. You may not stand to save as much as the world's richest people, but any savings is money that can work toward creating a better retirement.

The Disappearing Pension

What does an extinct automobile have to do with pensions? Quite a bit, actually. The Studebaker was a hot car back in the 1950s. It was sleek and fast. In many respects, it was ahead of its time, as it was the first production automobile to have such things as seatbelts and padded dashboards. They were reliable cars with style and power. But for some reason, the American public just fell out of love with them in the 1960s and the automaker fell on hard times. Studebaker was forced to close one plant after another and lay off thousands of workers. The last Studebaker rolled off the line on March 16, 1966.

In the middle of all of this, their executives discovered they had another major financial problem – their pension plans were poorly funded. They would not be able to keep their promises. Many of the laid-off workers, expecting their pensions to kick in, got zilch. Others received pennies on the dollar. Auto workers had a strong union, and they weren't about to take that lying down, so their union representatives complained loudly to Congress.

A general recession in the early 1970s caused other large corporations to default on their pensions. Congress responded with the Employee Retirement Income Security Act of 1974 (ERISA), which aimed to regulate pension plans. Now, it would be against the law to renege on pension promises. With the stricter regulations, companies just started phasing them out altogether.

A seismic shift was taking place when it came to the way Americans viewed retirement. It used to be you worked for the same company for thirty to forty years, and when you retired, you could count on a gold watch and a guaranteed pension check – usually a portion of your previous salary – coming in for the rest of your life. All that changed with pensions becoming an endangered species. With the birth of ERISA, there came something new called the do-it-yourself individual retirement account (IRA), and another program that sounded like a vitamin supplement – the 401(k), which could be sponsored and administrated by your employer. Congress created these to incentivize workers to put aside money themselves for their retirement. The incentive was tax-deferment. Every dollar you contributed to your plan (up to a limit set by the IRS) was a dollar that Uncle Sam didn't tax you on until you withdrew it. Pensions were called "defined-*benefit* programs." These new employer-sponsored plans were called "defined-*contribution* plans."

The main difference, of course, was that simple word, "guaranteed." The pension plans were supposed to be iron-clad, and were guaranteed by the companies that offered them for the life of the employee. You did nothing to manage them. These new plans were invested in the stock market, primarily in mutual funds. They were dependent on the returns of investments you selected. There are no guarantees with 401(k)-type plans.

So there was good news and bad news. The good news was these plans allowed investments to grow tax deferred. With no taxes coming out, the account could accrue interest quicker and compounding was accelerated. The bad news was that you were now responsible for managing your own investments. During market crashes, such as the one that occurred in 2008, retirement accounts are hit with losses just like the rest of the stock market. For someone on the cusp of retirement, that can be a big "ouch!"

Tax-deferred is not tax-free, either. Uncle Sam is no fool. The government will get its slice of the pie (and it hopes a much bigger one) when the time comes for you to withdraw the money. And just to make sure you *do* withdraw the money, the government put something in place called required minimum distributions (RMDs), which forced you to withdraw an ever-increasing percentage of these tax-qualified accounts as soon as you reached age seventy-two.

IRAs have become very popular. Millions of Americans have pumped trillions of dollars into them. IRA owners were delighted to see their taxes shrink and their retirement savings compound quicker during the accumulation phase of their lives. But when they enter the distribution phase of retirement, or what I prefer to call the harvesting phase, they discover the IRA has a little more complexity than they first imagined. Passing their assets on to their heirs can be tricky. If you don't do it intelligently, the IRS can claim almost half of it for the tax coffers.

In 2019 the SECURE Act caused some big changes in the world of IRAs. In addition to pushing back the RMD age from seventy-and-one-half to seventy-two, this Act overhauled the rules on inherited IRAs. In the past, individuals who inherited an IRA were able to stretch the assets within the account over their lifetime. There were very few requirements on how quickly you had to withdraw these funds. Now you are required to withdraw everything in the account within ten years, unless you are the surviving spouse, a minor child, disabled, chronically ill, or less than ten years younger than the person who held the IRA.

The part of the Internal Revenue Service code that deals with IRAs is Publication 590, or "Pub 590" for short. The document is 110 pages long and contains the latest rules for IRAs. Ed Slott, a leading IRA expert, writes in his book, *"The Retirement Savings Time Bomb... and How to Defuse It,",* "Due to a complex combination of distribution and estate taxes that kick in at retirement or death, millions of you are at risk of losing much – perhaps even most – of your retirement savings."

Variations Emerge

Over time, Congress has enacted legislation that has created variations in tax-deferred retirement accounts such as IRAs, 401(k)s, 403(b)s and the like. The most significant has been the emergence of the *Roth* IRA and **Roth** 401(k), named for the late U.S. Sen. William V. Roth, a fiscal conservative who sponsored the legislation. Sen. Roth also co-authored the Economic Recovery Tax Act of 1981. He maintained that the less we have to pay in taxes, the more we will spend and save, which would, in turn, stimulate the economy. This, he claimed, would generate more revenue for the government in the long run than a direct tax would. The Taxpayer Relief Act of 1997, which was his idea, allows you to pay the taxes on the front end of a Roth IRA and 401(k), which in turn allows your investments to grow and be distributed tax-free. Today, Roth IRAs can be set up at many financial institutions and insurance companies, and more and more employers are offering Roth 401(k)s. They allow for early withdrawal of your original contribution (not the earnings) without penalties after a five-year waiting period. The earnings generated from the original Roth IRA contribution can also be withdrawn early, but they are subject to penalties.

I have given you a broad-brush explanation here. Rules are constantly changing, so see me in person or anyone at Advantage Retirement Group for a more detailed explanation or to answer any questions you may have.

Stay Focused on Your Goal

Keep in mind, retirement is the extended voyage you have longed to take on a cruise ship. It's a time to remain alert and keep your focus. During the accumulation phase of your financial life, you work hard to put money into the aforementioned accounts. You watch it grow, and hopefully reach your savings goal. When the preservation and distribution phase kicks in, you want to keep as much as you can of what you have earned and use the amount you need to maintain your current lifestyle. Since the rules are constantly changing, it will pay to be diligent in keeping up with them or having a financial navigator who knows what types of accounts exist and can advise you about using them.

CHAPTER EIGHT

Replacing the Disappearing Pension

Back when I first got into the financial services profession in 1983, cellular phones and the internet didn't even exist! If someone said "cable TV" you thought they meant that wire that went from the television to the outside antenna!

Nowadays, we are living in the information age. Or, as I call it, the information *overload* age. I mean, we are inundated with opinions from every angle. Talking heads on the financial channels seem to make a sport out of disagreeing with one another on what you should and shouldn't do with your money.

In previous times, you worked for a certain number of years, and you saved a certain amount of money and you *knew* how much you would have for retirement. Not so today. These days, you have to invest prudently and keep on top of it, because you are responsible. You've got to do it right. During the accumulation phase, when you are working, you are putting your wealth in the hopper, so to speak. You are going to invest differently in that phase because you are still working. But when you retire – and this is what a lot of people don't seem to understand fully – you will be taking the fruits of your labor and endeavoring to make sure they last as long as you do.

That's one of the reasons we call our radio and television shows "Saving the Investor." Saving the investor from what? From the possibility they will fall prey to the dangers of bad advice, bad timing, and bad decisions that could threaten their financial security. You don't want to have to go back to work, yet that is what many have to do who have not planned properly.

The tsunami of information spouted by the media can overwhelm rather than educate. Through additional platforms, more financial takes are disseminated by more people. Our goal on "Saving the Investor" is to cut through the fog with straight talk and common sense.

In the previous chapter of this book, we talked about disappearing pensions. If you have a pension, then consider yourself one of the fortunate few. Most of the people I meet with these days know what they are because their father or grandfather had one. Or they know someone who retired with a pension. These days, the adage comes to mind: If it is to be, it's up to ME! That's right, you have to find a way to create your own pension – or guaranteed lifetime income – if the company you work for hasn't seen fit to provide you with one.

Also, in the previous chapter, we discussed at great length why IRAs and 401(k)-type plans are great, but they are not pensions. Why? Because they are not guaranteed for life. One of the most common vehicles for creating your own guaranteed lifetime income stream, similar to a pension, -is the annuity.

Annuity Bias

Some people swear by them and some people swear at them, but there is nothing scary about annuities. They are merely a financial tool like so many others that can be used to provide a financial strategy to help solve a problem – in this case, the need for a lifetime income stream. So why is it that when you say the "A" word, some people want to hide under a rock, or worse, pick up the rock and try to hit you with it?

In my experience, we mostly fear what we don't understand.

Just for fun, I once asked an audience I was giving a talk to about income planning what they would think of a financial product that would perform the following functions:

- Provide protection of principal from market losses
- Offer tax-deferred interest earnings to accelerate growth
- Link interest earnings to upside market performance
- Hold its value and not go down when the market declined
- Provide an option for guaranteed lifetime income in retirement
- Potential to pass an unused portion to heirs upon one's death
- Potential to avoid probate process

When I asked for a show of hands as to how many would like a financial product such as the one I had just described, almost every hand went up. Then, I asked how many in the room liked annuities, and only a few hands went up. What I had described to them was a fixed index annuity with an income rider attached – a perfectly good solution to a financial problem in some cases.

When I asked why some did not raise their hands before they knew that what I had just described was an annuity, the answers I received told me that this audience was probably representative of most individuals – they simply did not understand them. Granted, they are not for everyone, but it doesn't hurt to understand how they work.

An Explanation and History

Origin – The word "annuity" comes from the Latin words "annu" or "annus," which means "yearly" or "annually." We get our English words "annual" and "anniversary" from the same root.

In the days of ancient Rome, soldiers pooled their money before going into battle so their widows and children would be cared for if they died. Paying the money out in a lump sum was life insurance, although they didn't call it that. Paying the money out in payments for the lifetime of the family was an annuity.

An annuity is a contract purchased by an individual from an insurance company. An annuity is typically used in retirement to secure an income for the remainder of your life, or to pay a fixed number of payments over a set period of time. Not all annuities are the same. A good example would be that all annuities are contracts, but not all contracts are annuities. All Fords are automobiles, but not all automobiles are Fords. Some annuities are as different from each other in what they do as a motorcycle is from a dump truck.

There are three basic ways to categorize an annuity:

1. Is it **fixed** or **variable?** This determines **how the annuity earns interest or is invested.** Fixed annuities are considered "safe" because the principal is protected by the insurer. Variable annuities are invested indirectly in the stock market, and the principal is exposed to market risk, just like any other market investment.

2. Do you want income **now** or **later?** This establishes if the annuity, and thus the income, is deferred (income later) or immediate (income now).

3. Is the annuity **single premium**, or **flexible premium?** This determines whether additional funds can be added to the contract.

There are four parties to an annuity:

The contract owner. The contract owner is the person who has purchased the annuity. The contract (annuity) owner:

- Pays the premium for the annuity.
- Signs the application and agrees to abide by the terms of the contract.
- Chooses who the other parties of the contract will be.
- Can withdraw money from the contract (according to the terms).
- May add funds to the contract if it is a flexible annuity.
- Is responsible for any taxes that are due when such withdrawals are made.
- May terminate the contract.
- Is responsible for selecting contract options from an available selection.
- May change beneficiaries.

The annuitant. This can be a little confusing. The annuitant *can* be the contract owner but does not have to be. Think of the annuitant in terms of life insurance. With life insurance, if the person who is insured dies, then the contract terminates. With an annuity, the annuitant is the *measuring life* of the contract. An annuitant is the person to whom annuity payments are made and during whose life an annuity is payable. So, until the contract owner makes a change, or until the person named as annuitant dies, the terms of the annuity remain in force. The annuitant, then, is like the insured in a life insurance policy. The annuitant can be anyone: you, a spouse, parent, child, or other relative. The annuitant must be an individual with a calculable lifespan, so it cannot be a trust, corporation, or partnership.

The insurer. An annuity is always a contract between an individual or individuals, or a trust, and an insurance company (the insurer). This applies whether you buy the annuity through an independent agent, a bank, or directly from the insurance company. The contract governs what can and cannot be done with the money you placed with the insurance company and the benefits you stand to receive from the contract. The wording in the contract will also spell out the rates, guarantees, limitations, costs, and charges, as well as any rules governing premium payments and withdrawals.

The beneficiary. The beneficiary of an annuity is similar to beneficiaries of other investments or insurance policies. Upon the annuitant's death, the beneficiary receives the contract's specified death benefit. The beneficiary cannot change or control the contract. He or she has no say in how funds are allocated (if applicable). The beneficiary only benefits from an annuity upon the annuitant's death. A beneficiary can be a child, spouse, friend, relative, trust, corporation, or partnership. An annuity can have multiple beneficiaries with varying percentages payable to each, equaling 100 percent. The contract owner can change beneficiaries at any time and the consent of a beneficiary is not necessary for changes to be made.

Types of Annuities

Annuities can be split into two main categories: *immediate* and *deferred*.

A deciding factor for choosing the annuity type you want will be based on your income needs and the flexibility desired. Do you want income now or in a few years? Do you want access to a lump sum of money? Would you like the most possible income? These are just a few of the questions you would need to think through before purchasing an annuity.

Immediate Annuity

If you purchase an immediate annuity, you are essentially trading a lump sum of money for an income stream. For example, you may give an insurance company $100,000 in return for, say, $500 per month for the rest of your life – regardless of how long you live. The amount of income would be based on your age and gender.

You also could have payments sent to you for a specified number of years. The amount of income would be based on interest rates and the number of years you want income. In any case, you can have the checks sent to you monthly, quarterly, semi-annually, or annually. (I am not a big fan of this type of annuity. I think you lose too much control. Once you trade your lump sum of money for an income stream, the insurance company does not allow you to access the remaining funds.)

Deferred Annuity

Deferred annuities are contracts designed to provide you with supplemental income for retirement or other long-term needs. The flexibility of deferred annuities, whether fixed or variable, is the main attraction.

With deferred annuities, there are three different types you can use depending on your needs and long-term objectives. You can purchase a fixed rate, fixed index, or variable annuity.

With most deferred annuities, there is a period of time during which the funds can be subject to surrender charges. The charges are incurred only if funds are withdrawn in excess of the free withdrawal percentage stipulated by your contract. Most annuities allow the owner to withdraw up to 10 percent each year without incurring a surrender charge. The surrender charge period is stated in the contract and is typically five to 10 years. The surrender charge gradually decreases to zero over the specified period. Withdrawals will reduce the contract value and will be subject to ordinary income tax and, since, as I said, this is designed for the long term, if you withdraw your funds before age fifty-nine-and-one-half, you might be subject to an additional 10 percent tax penalty.

Deferred Annuity Types

As I mentioned earlier, there are three types of deferred annuities: fixed rate, fixed index, and variable. Let's look at the basics of each.

Fixed-Rate Annuities

Like other fixed-rate products, a fixed-rate annuity provides the contract owner with a guaranteed rate of interest. When you purchase a fixed- rate annuity, generally, the longer the commitment, the higher the interest rate. The interest rates on fixed-rate annuities will vary from insurance company to insurance company. Annuity guarantees are backed by the financial strength of the insurance company and its ability to pay claims.

The most common time horizons for fixed-rate annuities are one, three, or five years. When you purchase a fixed-rate annuity, the interest rate is locked in for a specified time. The interest the annuity earns can be withdrawn by the contract owner (subject to limitations) or left in the annuity to maximize interest compounding.

Fixed-rate annuities are popular with individuals who want to keep their principal protected from market losses. With this type of annuity, you will know exactly what to expect each year in interest. Fixed-rate annuities can work well for conservative investors or those who want to know exactly what they will have earned at the end of a specific timeframe.

Fixed Index Annuities

Fixed index annuities combine the protection of principal with interest earnings linked to a market index (such as the S&P 500, Dow Jones, NASDAQ, Russell 2000, EURO STOXX 50, etc.). Fixed index annuities have been offered in the U.S. since the mid-1990s. They have many of the features of most fixed-rate annuity contracts except that the interest a contract earns is determined by the performance of an external index to which the annuity is linked. While the annuity is not actually participating in the market, when the index performs well, interest can be credited up to a predetermined amount, called a "cap," based on that performance. This interest is generally calculated once each year, on the annuity anniversary date.

Capped interest credits are one of the tradeoffs for no losses due to market declines If the market index goes up 20 percent in one year, your capped interest may be only 6 percent, but you are insulated from losses if the market loses 30 percent the following year. This protects your base. In a fixed index annuity, the worst you can do in a given year is make zero percent. This protection is why fixed index annuities have been popular with consumers as of late.

One main drawback of fixed index annuities is their complication. There are more than a few moving parts in this financial instrument. There are several methods for calculating interest, for example. The fine print is not necessarily damning, there is just a lot of it. This has steered many away from using them. If you decide to use a fixed index annuity, choose one that is easy for you to understand and make sure your financial advisor explains it thoroughly to your satisfaction. If you are moving a large amount of money, and if that money represents years of your hard work, your blood, sweat, toil, and tears, then make sure you understand where you are putting it and why you are putting it there. You should be as comfortable with that decision as you are that your left foot is in your left shoe. Make sure your advisor explains all the details and can supply in writing the answers to all your questions.

Variable Annuities

For individuals who have a higher risk tolerance, variable annuities offer an alternative. When you invest in a variable annuity, you control how your funds are invested in the annuity. Under the umbrella of a tax-deferred annuity there are usually many types of separate accounts (i.e. which invest in underlying mutual funds) in which to invest. The contract owner can allocate their money from sub-account to sub-account. (Some variable annuity contracts limit the frequency of movements.) With a variable annuity, you typically are investing in the stock market or bonds; therefore, there is risk of loss. If the investment does well, you receive all the benefit minus any fees. If the investment performs poorly, you can lose gains and even principal. In addition to surrender charges and possible income tax penalties, there are several fees associated with a variable annuity. Most have mortality and expense risk charges, sub-account expenses, and administrative fees. These fees can vary from one variable annuity to another and can be very costly.

These fees can come as a big surprise if you are unaware of how they are derived. One of my clients had a variable annuity and he was absolutely sure that he was paying no fees. As it turns out, his advisor did not explain it to him. We called the company and he listened firsthand as the company representative on the other end of the line explained to him that his $500,000 variable annuity was costing him 4.7 percent in fees, or almost $25,000 per year. That amounted to almost $250,000 over a 10-year period.

Which Annuity May Be Right for You?

The fact is that fixed-rate, fixed index, and variable annuities are all very popular. Annuities are not appropriate for everyone and will depend on your time horizon, your other current investments, your goals and objectives, and your personal risk-tolerance level.

Unfortunately, annuities have been given a bad name. I've found many advisors who try to use them as a one-size-fits-all solution. Before even thinking about an annuity, we go through a series of questions to understand your income needs. It's important to keep an open mind when considering whether annuities are a good option for your situation. Many annuity alternatives can avoid market risk while still ensuring growth. They can be less expensive and have a higher potential rate of return than other investments. Annuities are a tool that could be a great fit for part of a retirement plan when there is an income gap, either now or in the future. So don't count them out.

As all financial vehicles do, annuities have pros and cons. Take your time and clearly know why you are choosing any investment or insurance vehicle. Work with an advisor you trust, who will be patient enough to answer all of your questions. I believe if annuities are used correctly and in the right circumstances, annuities can be a very useful tool for part of your retirement.

CHAPTER NINE

The Problem
With *Average*
Returns

Wall Street and Main Street have different ways of calculating average rates of return. This could be a major deal breaker during your retirement years. If you are an investor looking for a secure retirement, this might be one of the most important chapters in the book, because it exposes the Wall Street method of calculating average returns.

Mutual funds are well known for calculating their annual returns on an *average* basis over five-year, ten-year, fifteen-year, and twenty-year periods of time, or even since the fund's inception date. After you read this chapter, I think you will see how crucial it is to think carefully about picking funds based on these calculations.

The Tale of Two Accounts

Let's pretend you have two accounts, each with a cool $1 million at your disposal to invest. With Account A you pick a very hot company and buy $1 million worth of its stock and it returns an astounding 60 percent.

With Account B, you are more careful. This is a diversified portfolio that didn't do too badly either – it only returned 30 percent. You are on a roll! But, as the old saying goes, what goes up must come down.

The second year, your hot stock that was up 60 percent takes a beating and Account A loses 40 percent. Your diversified portfolio, Account B, fares better, losing only 10 percent.

Now, let's do the math for account A: 60 percent minus 40 percent equals 20 percent, right?

Now for account B: 30 percent minus 10 percent equals 20 percent.

Both accounts *averaged* a 10 percent annual gain (20 percent divided by two years). But look at the accounts more closely. Account A started with $1 million. The gain of 60 percent put the account up to $1.6 million after year one. Account B started with $1 million, but had a 30 percent gain, which put the account up to $1.3 million after year one. Then both accounts had a setback. Account A lost 40 percent, so if we take 40 percent from $1.6 million, it leaves account A with $960,000.

Account B lost 10 percent. Take 10 percent from $1.3 million, which leaves us $1.17 million.

Two accounts had the same *average* rate of return but experienced very different outcomes. Wall Street calculates average rates of return by dividing the returns by the number of years the funds have been in existence. This is what I call "fuzzy math." That doesn't help you make sure the accounts you are choosing for your retirement or investments are the appropriate ones, does it? The fact that the *average* was the same on both accounts had no bearing on the outcome of your money inside those accounts.

Averages can be tricky.

If I put one foot in ice water and the other in hot water, on *average* I'm comfortable, right? No, I'm not!

I saw a cartoon once of a man wading across a pond. The sign at the edge of the water said, "Average Depth: 3 feet." The man was struggling to keep his head above water, however, because he had stepped into a hole. Sure, the *average* depth may have been 3 feet, but the man was drowning, nonetheless.

And If I tell you that Bob and Susan ride their bikes an average of seventy miles per week, you may get the *impression* of a lovely couple riding their bikes together down a shady country lane. However, the *reality* may be that Susan rides twenty miles every day while Bob sleeps late. Red flags go up when I hear the words "average" and "returns" in the same sentence.

Let's take ourselves back in time from 2000 to 2021. Why would we pick those years? I'm about to show you. But first, let me ask you a question. If I were going to demonstrate the performance of a particular portfolio, would you say it would be more accurate to pick the best twenty-plus years, or the twenty-plus years that would represent both the good times and the bad times too? The latter, of course.

Portfolio 1 is an account that is an index fund that tracks the S&P 500. It has low fees. Portfolio 2 has much higher fees but is a well-diversified account. Both accounts have had very similar returns during the twenty-first century. The S&P 500 index fund (Portfolio 1) returned 9.13 percent over that twenty-two-year period, and the well-diversified portfolio had an 8.69 percent return. Many people, because they want to be comfortable with what they're getting into, would lean toward the S&P 500 index. It has been around for a long time, and the fees are low compared to Portfolio 2. But would that be the best decision?

Consider the volatility that factors into each portfolio. The S&P index comprises large-cap stocks, which subject an investor to additional risk. Portfolio 2, meanwhile, contains large-cap, small-cap, and international stocks, along with a potential mix of bond funds. As you can see below in comparing the two portfolios when not withdrawing funds, the returns are about the same. However, stark differences in the portfolios can arise when taking income for retirement. In the examples below, I account for a $50,000 withdrawal each year. Greater volatility within Portfolio 1, which incorporates just S&P 500 large-cap stocks as the only asset class, resulted in an ending balance in 2021 totaling just under $400,000. Now, compare that with the 2021 ending balance in Portfolio 2, which reflects a slight gain above the initial investment ($1 million).

Why is that? It is nice to have other assets within a portfolio that may not decline as fast as stocks in the down years and could even increase in value. These additional asset classes can provide a buffer for the portfolio's equities and give those equities a chance to rebound faster when market conditions improve.

The bottom line is you don't want to take money out of a declining asset. We were able to re-position how we took income from Portfolio 2 because it contains fixed assets that were not declining at the same pace in lean years as Portfolio 1, comprised entirely of stocks.

When the market is rising, you can withdraw more from equities within a portfolio. But when the market is faring poorly and you need to take income, you want to take money from less volatile investments within the portfolio. Market performance can be unpredictable and you want a cushion to prevent the kinds of severe losses reflected in Portfolio 1. Even as we published this book in 2022, the year began with substantial market turbulence caused by rising inflation and the response by investors concerned with whether the Federal Reserve Board could combat that surge.[22]

---

[22] William Watts. marketwatch.com. January 10, 2022. "Why New Year's chaos may signal a more balanced—but volatile—stock market in 2022 as investors grapple with a hawkish Fed" https://www.marketwatch.com/story/why-new-years-chaos-may-signal-a-more-balanced-but-volatile-stock-market-in-2022-as-investors-grapple-with-a-hawkish-fed-11641653191

VOLATILITY VS. RETURNS – WHICH IS MORE IMPORTANT?

			Portfolio 1		
Year	Gains	Beg. Bal.	Earnings	Withdraw	End Bal.
2000	-9.10%	$1,000,000	-$91,200	$0	$909,000
2001	-11.89%	$909,000	-$108,080	$0	$800,920
2002	-22.10%	$800,920	-$177,003	$0	$628,917
2003	28.68%	$623,917	$178,939	$0	$802,856
2004	10.88%	$802,856	$87,351	$0	$890,207
2005	4.91%	$890,207	$43,709	$0	$933,916
2006	15.79%	$933,916	$147,465	$0	$1,081,381
2007	5.49%	$1,081,301	$559,368	$0	$1,140,749
2008	-37.00%	$1,140,749	-$422,077	$0	$718,672
2009	26.46%	$718,672	$190,161	$0	$908,832
2010	15.06%	$908,832	$136,870	$0	$1,045,702
2011	2.11%	$1,045,702	$22,064	$0	$1,067,767
2012	16.00%	$1,067,767	$170,843	$0	$1,238,610
2013	32.39%	$1,238,610	$401,186	$0	$1,639,795
2014	13.69%	$1,639,795	$224,488	$0	$1,864,283
2015	1.38%	$1,864,283	$25,727	$0	$1,890,010
2016	11.96%	$1,890,010	$226,045	$0	$2,116,055
2017	21.83%	$2,116,055	$461,935	$0	$2,577,990
2018	-4.39%	$2,577,990	-$112,916	$0	$2,465,074
2019	31.49%	$2,465,074	$776,252	$0	$3,241,326
2020	18.40%	$3,241,326	$595,432	$0	$3,836,758
2021	28.71%	$3,836,758	$1,101,533	$0	$4,938,291

Average Return: 9.13%, Standard Deviation: 17.88%

DISCLAIMER: *The above table is intended to illustrate the potential results of a hypothetical investment of $1,000,000 in a hypothetical investment that mirrors the performance of the S&P 500 index beginning on the first trading day of 2000 and held through the last trading day of 2020. This example is for illustrative purposes only and it is not possible to invest in the index itself. It is assumed that any dividends and other earnings are reinvested and no allowances for external advisory fees have been made. The results may vary significantly if the beginning day and/or the ending day is altered. The holdings composing the fund have changed over time and are likely to change in the future. Past performance is not indicative of future results.*

VOLATILITY VS. RETURNS – WHICH IS MORE IMPORTANT?

		Portfolio 2			
Year	Gains	Beg. Bal.	Earnings	Withdraw	End Bal.
2000	-6.64%	$1,000,000	-$66,400	$0	$933,600
2001	-6.98%	$933,600	-$65,165	$0	$868,435
2002	-12.46%	$868,435	-$108,207	$0	$760,228
2003	30.13%	$760,228	$229,057	$0	$989,284
2004	14.50%	$989,284	$143,446	$0	$1,132,731
2005	10.07%	$1,132,731	$114,066	$0	$1,246,797
2006	13.74%	$1,246,797	$171,310	$0	$1,418,106
2007	10.65%	$1,418,106	$151,028	$0	$1,569,135
2008	-30.98%	$1,569,135	-$486,118	$0	$1,083,017
2009	30.51%	$1,083,017	$330,428	$0	$1,413,445
2010	16.89%	$1,413,445	$238,731	$0	$1,652,176
2011	-0.18%	$1,652,176	-$2,974	$0	$1,649,202
2012	14.94%	$1,649,202	$246,391	$0	$1,895,593
2013	21.71%	$1,895,593	$411,533	$0	$2,307,126
2014	5.91%	$2,307,126	$136,351	$0	$2,443,477
2015	0.62%	$2,443,477	$15,150	$0	$2,458,627
2016	8.98%	$2,458,627	$220,785	$0	$2,679,412
2017	20.53%	$2,679,412	$550,083	$0	$3,229,495
2018	-6.45%	$3,229,495	-$208,302	$0	$3,021,193
2019	23.51%	$3,021,193	$710,282	$0	$3,731,475
2020	18.70%	$3,731,475	$697,786	$0	$4,429,261
2021	13.55%	$4,429,261	$600,165	$0	$5,029,426

Average Return: 8.69%, Standard Deviation: 14.87%

DISCLAIMER: *The above table is intended to illustrate the potential results of a hypothetical investment of $1,000,000 in a hypothetical mix of securities, which could yield a series of returns that are less volatile than the returns of an investment intended to track the S&P 500 over the same time period, beginning on the first trading day of 2000 and held through the last trading day of 2020. The results may vary significantly if the beginning day and/or the ending day is altered. The buildings composing the fund have changed over time and are likely to change in the future. The table does not represent the results of an investment of an actual security or mix of securities.*

THE IMPACT OF VOLATILITY WHEN TAKING INCOME

Year	Gains	Beg. Bal.	Portfolio 1 Earnings	Withdraw	End Bal.
2000	-9.32%	$1,000,000	-$93,200	-$50,000	$856,800
2001	-11.64%	$856,800	-$99,732	-$50,000	$707,068
2002	-22.06%	$707,068	-$155,979	-$50,000	$501,089
2003	28.03%	$501,089	$140,455	-$50,000	$591,544
2004	10.97%	$591,544	$64,892	-$50,000	$606,437
2005	4.64%	$606,437	$28,139	-$50,000	$584,576
2006	15.94%	$584,576	$93,181	-$50,000	$627,757
2007	5.59%	$627,757	$35,092	-$50,000	$612,849
2008	-37.13%	$612,849	-$227,551	-$50,000	$335,298
2009	24.14%	$335,298	$80,941	-$50,000	$366,239
2010	14.20%	$366,239	$52,006	-$50,000	$368,245
2011	2.45%	$368,245	$9,022	-$50,000	$327,267
2012	16.63%	$327,267	$54,424	-$50,000	$331,691
2013	33.00%	$331,691	$109,458	-$50,000	$391,149
2014	12.86%	$391,149	$50,302	-$50,000	$391,451
2015	0.86%	$391,451	$3,366	-$50,000	$344,817
2016	10.65%	$344,817	$36,723	-$50,000	$331,541
2017	21.88%	$331,541	$72,541	-$50,000	$354,082
2018	-4.38%	$354,082	-$15,509	-$50,000	$288,573
2019	31.49%	$288,573	$90,872	-$50,000	$329,444
2020	18.40%	$329,444	$60,618	-$50,000	$340,062
2021	28.71%	$340,062	$97,632	-$50,000	$387,694

Average Return: 8.91%, Standard Deviation: 17.79%

DISCLAIMER: The above table is intended to illustrate potential results of a hypothetical investment of $1,000,000 in a hypothetical investment that mirrors the performance of the S&P 500 index, beginning on the first trading day of 2000 and held through the last trading day of 2020. This example is for illustrative purposes only. It is not possible to invest in the index itself. It is assumed that any dividends and other earnings are reinvested and no allowances for external advisory fees have been made. The results may vary significantly if the beginning day and/or the en ending day is altered. The holdings composing the fund have changed over time and are likely to change in the future. Past performance is not indicative of future results.

THE IMPACT OF VOLATILITY WHEN TAKING INCOME

Year	Gains	Beg. Bal.	Portfolio 2 Earnings	Withdraw	End Bal.
2000	-6.64%	$1,000,000	-$66,400	-$50,000	$883,600
2001	-6.98%	$883,600	-$61,675	-$50,000	$771,925
2002	-12.46%	$771,925	-$96,182	-$50,000	$625,743
2003	30.13%	$625,743	$188,536	-$50,000	$764,279
2004	14.50%	$764,279	$110,820	-$50,000	$825,100
2005	10.07%	$825,100	$83,088	-$50,000	$858,187
2006	13.74%	$858,187	$117,915	-$50,000	$926,102
2007	10.65%	$926,102	$98,630	-$50,000	$974,732
2008	-30.98%	$974,732	-$301,972	-$50,000	$622,760
2009	30.51%	$622,760	$190,004	-$50,000	$762,764
2010	16.89%	$762,764	$128,831	-$50,000	$841,595
2011	-0.18%	$841,595	-$1,515	-$50,000	$790,080
2012	14.94%	$790,080	$118,038	-$50,000	$858,118
2013	21.71%	$858,118	$186,297	-$50,000	$994,416
2014	5.91%	$994,416	$58,770	-$50,000	$1,003,186
2015	0.62%	$1,003,186	$6,220	-$50,000	$959,405
2016	8.98%	$959,405	$86,155	-$50,000	$748,351
2017	20.53%	$748,351	$153,636	-$50,000	$851,987
2018	-6.45%	$851,987	-$54,953	-$50,000	$747,034
2019	23.51%	$747,034	$175,628	-$50,000	$872,662
2020	18.70%	$872,662	$163,188	-$50,000	$985,850
2021	13.55%	$985,850	$133,583	-$50,000	$1,069,433

Average Return: 8.69%, Standard Deviation: 14.87%

DISCLAIMER: The above table is intended to illustrate potential results of a hypothetical investment of $1,000,000, with $50,000 withdrawn from the investment annually, in a hypothetical mix of securities, which could yield a series of returns that are less volatile than the returns of an investment intended to track the S&P 500 over the same period, beginning on the first trading day of 2000 and held through the last trading day of 2020.. The results may vary significantly if the beginning day and/or the ending day is altered. The holdings composing the fund have changed over time and are likely to change in the future. The table does not represent the results of an investment of an actual security or mix of securities.

A well-designed strategic income plan is the most critical element to any retirement plan, particularly when counting on withdrawals from portfolios to supplement income. Again, just look at the staggering differences between the ending balances in the two hypothetical portfolios outlined.

When Wall Street is *averaging* these types of numbers, it doesn't matter to them when the positive or negative returns come, whether at the beginning of the time measured, or at the end. But should it matter to you? Yes, indeed! Especially if you are contemplating retirement! You don't want your portfolio to be caught with its proverbial pants down just after a recession whittles away a sizable chunk of what you have worked and saved so long and hard to accumulate, and now have to start withdrawing from at the very worst time. Now take a look back at the "Impact of Volatility When Taking Income" spread. Look what could have happened to these people's retirement in the S&P 500 index while taking out $50,000 each year for income.

Ask yourself, what would I have done if I had lost almost half my money after only a few years of retirement? How would it have affected me? Stockbrokers will sometimes say, "Just stay the course; it will come back." And they might be right! The stock market usually has rebounded (although no one can guarantee this) – eventually. But timing is crucial to retirees. If you stayed the course and rode it out like the income example shows, at the end of 2021, your $1 million portfolio would have been down to $387,694.

Let's take a look at the diversified portfolio that had the same average return as the S&P, even though the fees were higher. It *averaged* the same as the other portfolio, but it did not suffer near the amount of losses in the bad years and did not have near the high gains that the S&P index had.

Remember, Wall Street's *averaging* does not take your personal timeline into consideration. A market crash right at the time you retire could endanger your retirement security.

Conclusion: The *amount* of your return on your investments matters much more than the *rate* of return on your investments. You can't live on *average rates of return.* I like the way the famous American humorist Will Rogers put it during the Great Depression: "I'm not so concerned about the return *on* my money as I am about the return *of* my money."

CHAPTER TEN

Women On Deck

My wife Tommie loves the time she spends on our pleasure boat and enjoys opportunities we get to entertain friends. But do you realize there once was a time when sea captains would have considered the presence of a woman aboard a ship to be an affront to maritime superstitions?

Granted, it's understandable why certain omens became accepted when sailing the high seas centuries ago. Technology was primitive when compared to what we take for granted today, so seamen used their imagination to conjure good fortune.

Captains responsible for military vessels and merchant ships stubbornly held on to superstitions as tightly as they did the ship's wheel. Allow a woman on board, and the gods of the sea might angrily summon brutal waves and stormy weather.

Yet ships then and now are often referenced by the gender-specific pronouns she and her. From a historical perspective, Nina, one of the three Spanish ships used by Christopher

Columbus on his 1492 voyage to the Americas, is Spanish for "The Girl."

To this day, we frequently name boats after women, and I'm no different. I named my boat Tommie Jo, and we each smile every time we look at the lettering. We first became excited about boating in 2000 and learned boating is like a partnership. Both of us have our responsibilities and have to know the conditions that lie ahead. One example is docking the boat. Tommie quickly became comfortable and adept at handling the lines to either tie-off or hand-off when we head into different marinas. She helps put my mind at ease, especially since she's also a great navigator.

Recognizing those ancient and foolhardy concerns men had about letting women onboard, I sometimes wonder if a few men who come into our office arrived as passengers of a boat commanded by Columbus, Magellan, or Drake.

Or, it could be that Western traditions about money management being a "guy thing" prevailed in some households. You sense that mindset when couples visit our office, and the man of the house dominates conversations about retirement planning because he has mainly been responsible for investments and the handling of assets. Some husbands show up for an appointment without bringing their wives, a move we discourage.

A poll by the wealth management division of UBS found that 85 percent of women manage everyday expenses, but only 23 percent take the lead in long-term financial planning.[23] High net-worth women participated in the UBS study, and the vast majority identified future considerations – retirement planning, long-term care, and insurance – as their most vital financial needs.[24] Clearly,

---

[23] https://www.ubs.com/global/en/media/display-page-ndp/en-20190306-study-reveals-multi-generational-problem.html

[24] Ibid.

women deserve a spot at the table when mapping their finances. They also merit a spot at the conference table during discussions we have at Advantage Retirement Group.

Women outnumber men in the U.S. population.[25] In light of that statistic, it makes sense that women typically outlive men. In nautical terms, Mrs. Smith will likely be heading to a port that requires a more extended voyage than the lifelong cruise Mr. Smith is taking. The harsh reality is 80 percent of men die married, but 80 percent of women die single.

So, if you're the man of the house, what should the probability of you dying before your wife mean to you? Hopefully, you don't have to think too long. While your wife is grieving your death and tending to your memorial service and final wishes, she should be aware of every aspect within a comprehensive retirement plan – income, investments, taxes, health care, and legacy.

Every husband should want to leave his wife in the best position possible moving forward. It's going to be hard enough on her losing the lower of your two Social Security benefits, getting pushed in all likelihood into a higher tax bracket, and seeing little if no reduction in household expenses.

Typically, women have fewer personal resources to address the income gap they could face. Remember, women often spend more time out of the workforce providing unpaid care for younger children. It could be too that they devote time providing elder care to parents as those loved ones approach the ends of their lives.

Do you really want your wife to visit your advisor, wondering how all the dots in a financial plan connect, particularly if that advisor specializes only in investments? Women often fire their

---

[25] Statistica. 2021. "Total population in the United States by gender from 2010 to 2025" https://www.statista.com/statistics/737923/us-population-by-gender/

financial advisor after being widowed because many of them either feel disrespected or just plain didn't know their financial advisor.

We stress that every couple comes together and joins in at meetings we conduct while planning for retirement. Both the wife and husband should recognize all facets of retirement. Also, when they meet with me, I want them both to feel comfortable and trust that I am the right advisor to help them recognize and fulfill their retirement vision.

Going it alone is tough, even when things work out

Occasionally when a couple comes into the office, the wife attempts to establish a ground rule. She says something to the effect, "He takes care of everything; just talk to him." Early in my career, I would hear that sort of thing and not know how to respond.

Now I speak to the woman directly and say, "If we were all born on the same day, you're probably going to outlive us, maybe by a significant number of years." The responsibilities women potentially face after the death of their spouse can be overwhelming. Knowing beforehand how a comprehensive financial retirement plan works and knowing the financial professional who helped create that plan can be incredibly beneficial.

I want couples to understand each point I strive to make with complete clarity. If I need to back up, if I need to repeat myself, or if I need to word things differently, I'm more than happy to do so.

I am mindful of situations when women, still grieving over the loss of a husband, come to see us without much knowledge of the financial situation their husbands had monitored exclusively. Sometimes they don't know anything about the assets they had together. Often, such visits begin by looking into any life insurance policies in which the survivor is listed as the beneficiary to help with accessing those funds.

We've found too that when a husband exerts much of the financial decision-making, credit can become a key issue. Suppose the husband handles pretty much everything in terms of expenses. In that case, his surviving wife might have to apply for credit and have the ability to access different financial accounts.

Suppose any debt exists with, for example, a credit card or perhaps a car payment. In that case, it becomes necessary to send those creditors a copy of the death certificate and close out liabilities that were not the responsibility of the surviving spouse.

The resolution of debut can be just the beginning of a process aimed at resolving issues people face when attempting to understand the inner workings of an existing retirement plan in which they provided little input. It is sometimes prudent for the survivor to start from scratch in building a plan designed specifically for them.

Such plans might include establishing a lifetime income stream from an annuity and investing another portion of existing funds to help build and fortify accounts. Those investments can protect a survivor from potential hardships caused by thorny issues such as rising inflation and taxes. Collecting on the deceased spouse's Social Security, if it is the higher of the two Social Security benefits, is also appropriate and contributes to how the household copes without collecting two checks each month.

Legacy desires should also be addressed and involve introducing an estate planning attorney to help with an estate plan that takes care of children when the surviving spouse passes away.

This measure of steadfast assistance, which we attempt to provide through our Retirement Simulator Process, can be essential, especially in times of grief.

However, such sad occasions always make me think of the stress that could have been eliminated if financial matters had been explained before a loved one passed away. You never want to go at this alone, and by all means, finding a financial professional you like can be a relief.

While the story above references a married couple, single women with various retirement concerns visit our office all the time. Like anyone we meet with, we want to know what makes them tick and how they would best enjoy retirement.

Women face unique challenges in planning for retirement, a fact we especially find true with those who are single, whether they're divorced, widowed, or have been single their entire lives.

We've mentioned that women often live longer lives. They must make ends meet after often earning less during their working years than their male counterparts. The pay differential in our society has closed somewhat over time, yet among American workers in 2020, women earned eighty-one cents for every dollar men pocketed.[26]

---

[26] Kathleen Elkins. cnbc.com. July 18, 2020. "Here's how much men and women earn at every age" https://www.cnbc.com/2020/07/18/heres-how-much-men-and-women-earn-at-every-age.html

We have noticed women sometimes get categorized into what financial professionals call a "niche market" when describing their retirement needs. No. Women should never be relegated into a niche of any kind. Would you ever think of your mother as a niche? Certainly not. My mom happened to be the most instrumental person in my life.

It is important to us, though, to recognize some different characteristics and circumstances that can factor into retirement planning strategies designed for women. Our experience allows us to understand and better assist women for considerations they could face in retirement.

CHAPTER ELEVEN

Estate Planning: Do It for Love

I saw another clever comic strip the other day. All three frames had a drawing of a glass filled up halfway. Frame one read, "Optimist – the glass is half full." Frame two read, "Pessimist – the glass is half empty." Frame three read, "Estate Planning Attorney – The IRS took half because you didn't plan."

Nobody wants to think about death and dying, but dying is a fact of life. One of these days, we will join our ancestors. Like the old Hank Williams song says, "I'll never get out of this world alive." So the responsible, and loving, thing to do is plan for that eventuality. It is sensible from a financial point of view, and it makes life so much easier on those we leave behind if we take steps while we are living to communicate how we wish our assets to be transferred to our loved ones when we pass away. There are many advantages to taking care of this aspect of financial planning sooner rather than later. One is the potential to avoid probate.

What Exactly Is Probate?

The word "probate" comes from the Latin word *"probatum"* which means "providing proof." Probate is the legal process by which our worldly goods and possessions are distributed to others after we die. In an estate of some size, it becomes legally necessary to "prove the will" in a court of law before all who may have an interest in what we leave to whom. So why is it a problem?

You could say that probate is the traffic jam at the intersection of Last Will and Testament. It can become a protracted legal mess that frustrates your loved ones and makes lawyers wealthy. But, with a little planning, it doesn't have to be that way.

The law mandates that the courts in each state will govern the manner in which what you leave behind is distributed to your heirs. If the courts are involved, that means so are attorneys. Time delays can be expected. After all, the law doesn't say that the court has to be in a hurry to get this done.

How much time the probate process will take often depends on how complicated your estate is, and whether someone decides to contest your instructions. If the estate is complex, it can take years to settle things. The last time I checked, attorneys charge by the hour, and these fees are paid from your estate.

And another thing that makes us uneasy about probate – court proceedings are open to the public. That's right. Probate proceedings are often published, allowing anyone who wishes to peer into your family's private affairs. Some people think that probate only applies if you do not have a will. Not so. Whether or not you have a will, your estate will be subject to probate proceedings. The purpose of the process is to (a) pay your debts, and (b) distribute your assets to heirs and beneficiaries. That's one of the reasons probate proceedings are so public. That way, anyone who thinks your estate owes them something can file a claim against it. Aside from the invasion of privacy and embarrassment that could possibly result, the publicity can serve as a magnet for predators who come out of the woodwork once they hear of a large inheritance "on the block." Vendors, contractors, and attorneys representing private individuals can take issue with the provisions of the will and make claims against the estate.

If you have drawn up a will, you probably selected an individual to serve as your personal representative in these actions. If you die without a will, the court will determine that detail for you. Your personal representative will be responsible for inventorying all your property and worldly belongings so a value can be placed on your estate. Before your heirs get what you leave them, your estate will first discharge the following debts and obligations:

- Funeral expenses
- Estate administration costs, such as appraisal fees and advertising costs
- Taxes and ordinary debt
- All valid claims against the estate

It is not uncommon to see long delays between the filing of the will and the distribution of funds and property to heirs. One woman told me that her husband had passed away five years ago, and his estate was still in probate. When I asked her why, she said it was because his relatives were still squabbling over the assets. When there are disputes between family members (and it happens more often than you might think), the assets of the estate are frozen while accountants and appraisers calculate, to the penny, the value of the estate's inventory. All that takes time and money.

Avoiding the Probate Trap

All that sounds pretty dire, Alfie. Is there any way around it?

I'm glad you asked! As a matter of fact, there is! That is part of what estate planning is all about. Nearly all of the evils of probate can be eliminated, or at least reduced, through proper estate planning.

First, there are the psychological benefits. If you are like most people, you shudder at the thoughts of those you leave behind having to grieve in full view of the public, or having to worry about what the courts are doing with your estate. If you plan ahead, they won't be forced to watch as the probate process erodes the value of your estate. So, what are some of the strategies that can allow you to bypass the probate process?

Trusts – One way to avoid probate is to get rid of your property. That's essentially what trusts do – they rename your property so that it is no longer legally yours but belongs to an entity. The law allows you to control the entity, and this allows you to maintain control of your assets.

Another cartoon strip I saw on the subject of estate planning was a takeoff on the three little pigs and the big bad wolf. You know the story, of course. The big bad wolf blows down the houses of two of the pigs, because of their insubstantial construction. But the third pig's house, which was built of bricks, withstood the huffing and puffing of the lupine villain. In the cartoon, the three little pigs are shown huddled in a house made of stone blocks, each of which were labeled, "irrevocable trusts." The cartoon big bad wolf, of course, represented the taxman.

A living trust goes into effect while you are still alive. If it is revocable, it means you can change your mind. Irrevocable means you can't change your mind. For the purposes of protecting your property from the taxman and probate, irrevocable trusts are stronger and hold up better under legal pressure.

Sometimes revocable trusts become irrevocable when a person dies or becomes incompetent. The biggest difference between revocable and irrevocable trusts manifest when estate taxes are involved. When you place the property in an irrevocable trust, the property no longer belongs to you and is not considered part of your estate. You can see what a difference that would make in a large estate when it comes to determining how much your estate is subject to in death taxes. If you change your mind, you are returning the property to yourself, and it is considered part of your estate.

So why would anyone consider a revocable trust? What if the value of the estate is below the federal estate tax exemption, which in 2021 was $11.7 million? In that case, you may not need to be concerned. Those laws are subject to change, however. A revocable living trust is a written agreement that covers three phases of your life – (a) while you are alive and healthy, (b) if you should become incapacitated, and (c) after your death.

Also, you may be setting up a trust for the purposes of helping a charity. In that case, you may want an escape hatch that allows you to change your mind if your circumstances, or that of the charity, change.

The fact is, a properly prepared trust prevails legally over a last will and testament. A word of caution: Trusts must be prepared so as to comply with the laws of the state in which the estate dwells. Otherwise, your estate may not be properly protected. Any competent estate attorney will know how to properly prepare the trust to comply with state laws.

One more point – just having a trust is not enough by itself to avoid probate – you must *fund* the trust. That means you must actually change the names on the titles and deeds from individual names to the name of the trust. You must also make sure your beneficiaries to the trust are in place. That is what ensures the assets flow to those to whom you designate. To be probate-proof, the trust must own your assets. You can sign all the documents, but if you haven't funded the trust, it's an empty shell.

According to The Florida Bar, a statewide organization for Florida lawyers, a revocable trust "avoids probate by effecting the transfer of assets during your lifetime to the trustee. This avoids the need to use the probate process to make the transfer after your death. The trustee has immediate authority to manage the trust assets at your death; appointment by the court is not necessary."

Here's how the organization's website, www.floridabar.org, describes a revocable trust:

"A revocable trust is a document (the "trust agreement") created by you to manage your assets during your lifetime and distribute the remaining assets after your death. The person who creates a trust is called the 'grantor' or 'settlor.' The person responsible for the management of the trust assets is the 'trustee.' You can serve as trustee, or you may appoint another person, bank or trust company to serve as your trustee. The trust is 'revocable' since you may modify or terminate the trust during your lifetime, as long as you are not incapacitated.

"During your lifetime, the trustee invests and manages the trust property. Most trust agreements allow the grantor to withdraw money or assets from the trust at any time and in any amount. If you become incapacitated, the trustee is authorized to continue to manage your trust assets, pay your bills, and make investment decisions. This may avoid the need for a court-appointed guardian of your property. This is one of the advantages of a revocable trust.

"Upon your death, the trustee (or your successor, if you were the initial trustee) is responsible for paying all claims and taxes, and then distributing the assets to your beneficiaries as described in the trust agreement. The trustee's responsibilities at your death are discussed below.

"Your assets, such as bank accounts, real estate, and investments, must be formally transferred to the trust before your death to get the maximum benefit from the trust. This process is called 'funding' the trust and requires changing the ownership of the assets to the trust. Assets that are not properly transferred to the trust may be subject to probate. However, certain assets should not be transferred to a trust because income tax problems may result. You should consult with your attorney, tax advisor and investment advisor to determine if your assets are appropriate for trust ownership."

Beneficiaries – With some trusts, you can be the trust's beneficiary. That beneficiary line is one of the most important lines on many financial documents. When you say the word "beneficiary," most people think of life insurance. But many other documents, such as retirement savings accounts and IRAs, have designated beneficiaries.

I know of a case where a couple was married for ten years and then divorced. The woman had a good job at a software company and hundreds of thousands of dollars in her 401(k). Because she neglected to change the beneficiary line on her 401(k), when she died in an automobile accident, the money went to her ex-husband and not to her children.

In another case, a man failed to update his documents and left his former wife as the sole beneficiary on a $2 million life insurance policy when he remarried. Upon his death, his widow was left with nothing, while his former wife received the $2 million. Nothing could be done, because those beneficiary lines typically trump the provisions of a will.

In most cases, assets with designated beneficiaries do not have to go through the probate process. When I do document reviews for clients, one of the first things I look at is the beneficiary line. Would you believe that on some documents, hundreds of thousands of dollars are inadvertently set to be paid out to an ex-spouse? Just think of how that scenario would play out if the person who owned the assets remarries. By neglecting to update their documents, they would be disinheriting their current spouse.

I have seen some cases where the designated beneficiary line has been left blank. Sometimes it will say simply, "estate." I have also seen the word, "spouse," or "husband" or "children" on the beneficiary line. Make sure you designate your beneficiaries by name. You may wish to leave the asset first to your spouse, then equal shares to your children should your spouse die. If you don't have enough room to express all of that on the beneficiary line, use another sheet of paper and express your wishes fully. Make it clear so there will be no mistake as to what you intend. Remember, the idea of estate planning is to ensure that, when you die, your belongings and assets transfer to your heirs in the manner in which you intended while you were alive. For that to be the case, you must *legally express* your intentions.

Some account custodians may require a change of beneficiary form to update documents. These can usually be downloaded and printed out in a matter of minutes. If the beneficiary is a minor, you will need to designate an adult as an administrator of the funds. That administrator is usually the person your will names as guardian, but it does not have to be. You can also create a trust and name a trustee. Insurance companies don't write checks to minors.

Joint Ownership with Rights of Survivorship – One way to make clear who gets what in an estate is to use joint ownership with rights of survivorship. Investment accounts, for example, with TOD (transfer on death) designations, allow for naming beneficiaries and are not required to go through probate. If an asset has joint ownership with right of survivorship, it passes through to the second owner when the first owner passes away. If that asset contains a TOD provision, the assets pass along to the beneficiary if both joint owners die. Either way, the asset will probably not have to go through probate.

If an individual's name is on the document as co-owner, that person continues to own the asset when the other co-owner dies. Think of a joint checking account where both the husband and wife equally own and equally control the money in the account. There is no wrangling in a probate court as to who owns that asset. Likewise, it is the same with property or an investment account when it is articulated on the documents that the asset is owned by *joint tenants with rights of survivorship*, not as tenants in common. Please see your estate attorney on this one. Laws vary from state to state.

Do You Need a Trust?

Whether you need a trust depends on a number of circumstances. You may need to establish a trust if:

- You have a complicated family situation that requires adjusted timelines. An example would be that you wish to care for your spouse first, and upon his or her death you want the rest to go to your children from a previous marriage.
- You wish to leave your assets to your heirs in such a way that it is not immediately payable to them. For example, you may wish to leave it to a son or daughter in lump sums when they achieve a life goal, such as graduation, etc.

- A sizable portion of your assets are in real estate, or a business.
- You have an heir who suffers from a disability and you wish to provide for him or her without interrupting some type of government assistance. The trust would carefully dole the money out so as not to disqualify them.

Trusts can also be an effective tool in taking care of pets after you've died. It may sound silly, but I've seen pet care overlooked too many times, with heartbreaking results.

We love our pets. To many of us, our dogs, cats, birds (here in Florida: alligators, snakes, camels, llamas. . .) are part of the family. It's important, then, to give careful thought to guaranteeing their care in the event they outlive you. You must consider first, who is the best qualified to care for your pet(s)? And second, how do you expect them to be cared for?

I recommend talking to the person or persons whom you think would be a good fit for your pets. Make sure they're on the same page as you. In a trust, you can spell out your wishes. You might allocate a certain amount of money to be set aside for your pet's care and to pay for future medical bills. If you haven't experienced it already, take it from me—animal medical care can be outrageously expensive.

Some years ago, one of my family's dogs needed ACL surgery. It was not cheap. To make it worse, it's not like we had insurance to cover such a thing. (Pet insurance does exist, but most pet owners don't realize it or can't rationalize the expense.)

When I come home from a long day at work, nothing cheers me up like our three dogs, Katie, Chloe, and Tiger, greeting me with their undying enthusiasm. Animals have a sort of unconditional love that's unparalleled. To me, they deserve every bit of forethought to ensure they live out their days in comfort and happiness, even if it must be without you. If you agree, take some time to consider your pets when drafting a trust.

Powers of Attorney

Sam and Wanda (a hypothetical couple) are on vacation and they are involved in a serious automobile accident. They survive, but both are badly injured. While they will recover eventually, they learn they will have to stay in the hospital for six months or more.

Who is going to care for such things as their utility bills so the freezer stays on and the water pipes don't freeze? Who is going to collect and open their mail? If Sam and Wanda had the presence of mind to appoint someone they trust to act in their behalf, it will be no problem. It could be a son or daughter, or another trusted family member with the time and circumstances to perform the task. This is what long-term powers of attorney are for. Include such a document in your estate plan. Let the person you select for this duty know, and keep your documents in a fire-proof safe in your house.

Living Wills

When I ask clients if they have a living will, I sometimes get a blank stare. I know what they are thinking. "What is that?"

Let's face it, no one wants to talk about death and dying at a family gathering. But it is probably one of the most loving things you can do for your family. A living will expresses what you want to happen in the event you are not able to make life and death decisions for yourself. Living wills and medical directives specify health care and end-of-life decisions so your loved ones will not have to wring their hands over what you would want them to do. Along with the living will usually goes a health care power of attorney. This designates a loved one who knows you well to have the responsibility to instruct doctors and nurses if you are no longer cognizant of your surroundings. Some people want artificial life support. Others may wish to have some types of life support and not others. Some may want none at all. These documents do your speaking for you when you can no longer speak for yourself.

Remember the Terri Schiavo case? She was a St. Petersburg, Florida, resident who collapsed in 1990 and was rushed to the hospital where she remained in a coma for eight years, kept alive by machines. The doctor proclaimed her brain dead, but relatives struggled with what to do. The husband finally decided to have her feeding tube removed. That would have ended her life, but her parents fought the move. The matter was left for the courts to decide and dragged out for years with the entire nation watching.

Of course, the key question was, "What would Terri have wanted?" But no one knew. She did not have a living will, which would have settled the issue quickly and spared everyone all the anguish.

Health care professionals are relieved when they see that families have these documents. They will usually ask for them before a serious operation or when someone is admitted to the hospital. They respect the wishes of the individual, too. They are not just for the elderly and infirm. Anyone could have an accident or sudden illness at any time. It only makes sense, while you are planning, to include a living will and a durable health care power of attorney in your documents.

When You're the One Left Behind

I've read many books on financial planning, many of them written by my good friends and peers in this industry. They all cover the basics of protecting your spouse after you die. What few of them ever mention is what to do when you're the one who outlives your spouse.

Losing a loved one in death is always traumatic. Few losses rival the pain of having your husband or wife die. But it happens every day. I wish I could tell you how to deal with it, but there is no easy way to reconcile death nor to quickly overcome the feelings it evokes. I can, however, prepare you to deal with the financial quagmire that inevitably arises in the wake of a spouse's death.

The last thing you'll want to do while mourning is to wade through financial documents. It must be done, though; the repercussions of neglecting such action will be much more painful in the long run. If, at least, you know exactly what to do, it can substantially simplify the process.

Here are a few of the essentials—things you absolutely cannot forget to do. I recommend, however, that you consult with a financial advisor as a couple, long before one spouse dies, to arrange a more comprehensive list of "to-dos." It's not an easy conversation to have, but in the future, you'll be glad to have done it.

1) Do not make any big decisions like moving, buying large ticket items, or making major financial decisions. In the emotional time immediately after losing a spouse, it's easy to make impetuous choices. Take time to adjust and sit back to think carefully about the direction in which you want to go.

2) If your spouse was on Social Security, you must contact the administration and request they stop payments or transfer payments to you. If you do not do this, the SSA will come back and remove funds from your bank account.

3) You will need death certificates to transfer accounts to your name. Some entities will require original documents. Take

care to have exactly the documentation needed to save yourself some heartache.

4) If your spouse had IRAs, they will have to be put under your name.

5) If you are over age seventy-two, you will have to withdraw money from such accounts. The least you can take out is called the Required Minimum Distribution (RMD). Failure to withdraw RMDs results in painful fines.

6) Call all money accounts like brokerage and banks to transfer assets. This is only possible if you are listed in advance as joint owner on the accounts or as beneficiary on life insurance, annuities, and IRAs.

Again, this is just a cursory overview of what you must do after losing your spouse. There are likely other steps you'll need to take based on personal circumstances.

For example, a dear friend of ours lost her husband a few years back. He had several credit cards with outstanding debt. When she called to address the issue, two interesting things happened. First, she learned that she was not liable for the balance on his cards. That was an unexpected blessing. Second, though, she was told she could not transfer the card into her possession—her credit disqualified her. She needed to instead get her own credit card to start a line of credit.

Next, she set about turning in their second car, which was a lease. To her happy surprise, she was allowed to hand it over early without any fines.

Things worked out nicely for our friend, but that isn't always the case. When her husband died, she discovered that she knew very little of their financial situation. Better planning on their part could have ensured that she was clued into the family's finances and plans.

There's a sad reality of financial planning for couples: someone always has to die first. Often, it's the husband. Unfortunately, it is also often the husband who manages the couple's finances. Far too often, I've seen widows left up a creek without a paddle. It's a travesty, and it's unnecessary.

Estate Planning Fails

What follows are some examples of famous people who failed to plan their estates properly and the sometimes strange consequences that followed:

Michael Jackson: When the King of Pop died in 2009 of an overdose of propofol and benzodiazepine, he left behind an estate that was far from properly planned. It was estimated that he earned hundreds of millions per year, but he spent so extravagantly that it was unclear even to Jackson's closest advisors what his estate was worth. \

His Neverland Ranch cost millions each year. It contained an amusement park and a zoo, and took as many as 150 employees to keep it running. Jackson's debts were between $400 million and $500 million at the time of his death.

Jackson made implausible choices in planning his estate, choosing his aging mother to be the guardian of his children, and Diana Ross, famous former member of the Motown singing group, The Supremes, as a backup guardian. What if their grandmother died? Would the children then move in with Diana Ross?

Legal wrangling over his estate went on for years, though in 2021, a tax court judge valued three disputed elements of Jackson's estate at $111 million rather than the $482 million figure assignedby the IRS.[27]

While this proved to be a victory for Jackson's children, years of courtroom procedures could have been avoided with more prudent estate planning.

One problem with Jackson's estate was organization. He reportedly left so many investment accounts, bank accounts and documents scattered throughout the globe that getting a comprehensive snapshot of his entire estate was virtually impossible. The lesson here is to have an attorney pull your estate together for those you leave behind. Let trusted family members know where your important documents and assets are.[28]

James Gandolfini: When the star of the TV series "The Sopranos" died in 2013, his will directed his executors to pay any estate taxes that were due before his assets were divided up among his heirs. Liz Weston, writing in an article entitled, "Five Celebrities Who Messed Up Their Wills," which appeared Aug. 1, 2013, in MSN Money, said, "The problem is that any wealth left to his wife, Deborah Lin, could have avoided estate taxes entirely. (Although the federal estate tax can kick in on estates worth more than $5 million, you can leave an unlimited amount to a spouse without incurring a tax bill.)"

Anna Nicole Smith: The case of Vickie Lynn Marshall (stage name Anna Nicole Smith) will go down in history as one of the all-time estate nightmares. She was the former *Playboy* centerfold

---

[27] Andrew Dalton. Associated Press. May 5, 2021. "Michael Jackson's mother, children land major estate tax victory years after his death" https://www.usatoday.com/story/entertainment/celebrities/2021/05/05/michael-jackson-kids-mom-estate-tax-win-years-after-his-death/4952471001/

[28] Tim Lloyd. Wealth Management Today. March 5, 2015. "5 Epic Hollywood Estate Planning Fails." http://wmtoday.com/2015/03/05/5-epic-hollywood-estate-planning-fails/. Accessed Dec. 22, 2016.

who married 89-year-old billionaire oil tycoon, J. Howard Marshall II, whom she met at a strip club where she worked. Marshall died 13 months after the marriage. A court battle ensued when relatives claimed that Smith was not entitled to Marshall's considerable fortune. While Smith was fighting in probate court to claim a portion of Marshall's money, she died. Her will left everything to her teen son, who had died before she did. You can imagine what a mess this was. Making matters worse, Anna Nicole Smith also had a baby before she died. The child was essentially disinherited. The lesson we can learn here is to update your wills regularly – at least once a year. When significant family events occur, such as divorces, marriages, or births, re-structure your documents to accommodate them.

Gary Coleman: You may remember the wisecracking youngster from the TV show of the 1980s, "Diff'rent Strokes." When he died in Utah in 2010, he was not wealthy. He still had some acting royalties coming in, but he left behind conflicting wills and a puzzling note that sparked a court battle.

The first will filed in probate court was drafted in 1999, and left his estate to his former manager. The second will, signed in 2005, left everything to a friend. Adding to the confusion, he married Shannon Price in 2007 and amended the second will, making her his heir. The codicil was handwritten and included these strange words: "This I have done because of my personal selfishness and weakness and I love her with all of my heart." A year later, Coleman and Price divorced. That invalidated the codicil under Utah law, but Price argued that she should have inherited the estate, which consisted of a house with a mortgage and some modest assets, because they were living together even though divorced.

Coleman slipped and fell at his home and went into a coma. Price had been given power of attorney to make medical decisions if he were incapacitated. She ordered the doctors to disconnect life support a day after the fall. A court document later surfaced that showed the 42-year-old actor had asked that he be kept alive for at least 15 days in such circumstances. Clearly, Coleman had failed to update his estate plans after a major life event (marriage and then divorce). It is a lesson to make sure those to whom you issue power of attorney will carry out your wishes.

Marilyn Monroe: Marilyn Monroe died of what was reported as a suicide (sleeping pills) in 1962. Her will was probated in New York and the proceedings were not closed until 2001. What was the problem? When the famous actress died, she was unmarried and had no children. The problem was she had left the entire estate (with the exception of $100,000 to care for her mother) to her acting coach, Lee Strasburg. The estate is now in the name of Marilyn Monroe LLC and still makes millions of dollars per year for Strasburg's widow, who barely knew Monroe. Had the blond bombshell used a revocable living trust instead of a will, her heirs could have avoided a thirty-nine-year legal battle. She could also have specified that profits from her ongoing celebrity after her death would be payable to a specific person or charity.

Phillip Seymour Hoffman: Perhaps best known for his portrayal of Truman Capote, Phillip Seymour Hoffman died of a drug overdose in 2014 and left his estate worth $35 million to his partner and mother of his three children, Marianne O'Donnell. He neglected to create trusts for the children. Because the couple was not married, he created a $15-million tax event. Had O'Donnell and Hoffman tied the knot, the estate would have been transferred tax-free. By not setting up a revocable trust, Hoffman's estate was destined to end up on probate, exposing to the public all of the family's financial information.[29]

---

[29] John Goralka. Kiplinger. July 26, 2017. "Philip Seymour Hoffman's $12 Million Estate Planning Mistake." https://www.kiplinger.com/article/retirement/t021-c032-s014-philip-seymour-hoffman-s-estate-planning-mistake.html

These are just a few. The archives of Hollywood and the music world are strewn with examples of poor estate planning, procrastination, and, even worse, no estate planning at all. Getting your affairs in order requires a little time and effort while you are alive but can save your loved ones much anguish and time. Planning the details of the orderly transfer of your property after your death is one of the most loving gifts you could possibly present to your family.

Your estate plan is like an anchor. It serves to protect and preserve your wishes, so your assets are not, metaphorically speaking, washed out to sea, causing needless pain and tumult for your loved ones.

A SURVIVOR'S CHECKLIST

Things that need to be done when a loved one dies

Keep with your important papers

IMMEDIATE

☐ Obtain signed death certificate and autopsy records, if applicable.

☐ Within 24 hours, look for organ donation records. Check for signed authorizations and arrange immediately.

☐ Inventory safe deposit boxes and personal papers of the deceased. Look for burial insurance policies; prepaid mortuary or cremation society plans.

☐ Contact friends and relatives. ALLOW YOUR FRIENDS AND FAMILY TO HELP YOU OUT IN THIS TIME OF NEED.

☐ Make arrangements for pets (if any).

☐ Cancel regular elder assistance services.

☐ Obtain certified copies of the death certificate from the mortuary. Consider purchasing 10 to 20 copies.

WITHIN 30 DAYS

If applicable, notify:
- ☐ Social Security Administration to stop checks
- ☐ Department of Health Services if the deceased was receiving Medicaid
- ☐ Veterans Administration
- ☐ Payers of any pensions (such as former employer), or annuities
- ☐ Department of Motor Vehicles

Locate documents, including:
- ☐ Will
- ☐ Trust(s)
- ☐ Insurance policies
- ☐ Deeds to real estate

If there was a living trust, contact:
- ☐ Successor trustee (trust manager) for eventual distribution of assets
- ☐ **ADVANTAGE RETIREMENT GROUP** for review of possible death and/or income taxes owed, as well as assistance in sorting out and distributing assets
- ☐ Insurance companies and arrange for any death benefits to be paid to beneficiaries
- ☐ IRA and pension companies for any death benefits to be paid to beneficiaries

If there was no trust, and only a will, contact:
- ☐ County clerk and deposit the original will within 30 days
- ☐ Executor to begin the probate process with an attorney
- ☐ **ADVANTAGE RETIREMENT GROUP** for review of possible death and/or income taxes owed, as well as assistance in sorting out and distributing assets

WITHIN 60 DAYS

☐ Notify all creditors and utility companies
☐ Transfer title on jointly held assets
☐ Inventory personal effects and arrange for disposition
for family members, friends, or charities

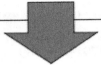

WITHIN SIX MONTHS

If surviving spouse:
☐ Contact **ADVANTAGE RETIREMENT GROUP** for review of finances and revised financial game plan (e.g.,
replace a lost pension, increase safety of remaining assets, etc.)
☐ Update your will or trust

CHAPTER TWELVE

Covering Long-Term Care

When CBS once aired a segment on the top retirement fears of American seniors, you could see the worry on the faces of the people they interviewed. One woman told the reporter, "I don't believe I'm comfortable with the amount we've saved." When the reporter asked her to explain, her response focused on unexpected medical expenses. She said she knew that medical bills could wreck a family budget.

Her late mother's savings dwindled to $11,000 when she developed Alzheimer's and spent her last five years in a nursing home.

"I've seen that the cost of care in a skilled facility is rising faster than salary or savings can possibly rise," she said. "So I need to be prepared for that because none of us want to leave that bill on our kids' shoulders."

According to the report, which aired in 2016, mind you, a couple will need approximately $220,000 to cover future medical costs.[30] Fast forward just five years to 2021, and a couple could need approximately $300,000, after taxes, to cover health care expenses in retirement.[31]

The Alzheimer's Association reports that 11.3 percent of those over sixty-five have the disease, and 34.6 percent of Americans age eighty-five and older had Alzheimer's dementia. The estimated lifetime cost of care for someone with Alzheimer's is $357,297.[32]

If those figures are even close to accurate, then, as the commander of the endangered space capsule Odyssey said to Mission Control in the movie "Apollo 13": "Houston, we have a problem." The median retirement savings of American households between the ages of fifty-five and sixty-four is $134,000. Consequently, the vast majority of retirees in the United States are drastically under-prepared for such an eventuality as long-term care.[33]

A good estate plan will consider the possibility of long-term care. What is the probability of your needing long-term care in the later years of your life? According to the LongTermCare.gov

---

[30] Anthony Mason. CBS Evening News. February 18, 2015. "The top retirement fear of American seniors." http://www.cbsnews.com/news/high-medical-expenses-top-u-s-retirement-fears/. Accessed Dec. 22, 2016.

[31] Fidelity.com. August 31, 2021. "How to plan for rising health care costs" https://www.fidelity.com/viewpoints/personal-finance/plan-for-rising-health-care-costs

[32] Care.com. November 30, 2020. "What is the lifetime cost of caring for a person with Alzheimer's?" https://www.care.com/c/lifetime-cost-alzheimers-care

[33] Alana Benson. MarketWatch.com. December 6, 2020. "Here are the average retirement savings by age: Is it enough?" https://www.marketwatch.com/story/here-are-the-average-retirement-savings-by-age-is-it-enough-2020-11-16

website, "someone turning sixty-five today has almost a 70 percent chance of needing some type of long-term-care services and supports in their remaining years. Women need care longer (3.7 years) than men (2.2 years). One-third of today's sixty-five-year-olds may never need long-term care support, but 20 percent will need it for longer than five years."[34]

Which would you say is a bigger threat to our retirement nest eggs – stock market risk or long-term care? I seldom hear people telling me their parents lost everything they had saved all of their lives due to a stock market correction. But losing it all because of a nursing home confinement is all too common, particularly since the median retirement savings for those fifty-five to sixty-four in our country is $120,000.[35]

Genworth, a Fortune 500 insurance company, surveys the cost of long-term care across the United States each year. Genworth's 2020 Cost of Care Survey (conducted by CareScout®), is the most comprehensive survey of its kind and covers over 55,000 long-term care providers in 440 regions nationwide. The annual median cost of a private room in a Florida nursing home was $117,804 and expected to experience an annual growth rate of 4 percent! It's easy to see how that could quickly wipe out a retirement nest egg in a hurry. Other median annual Florida long-term-care rates include:

- Homemaker services - $50,340
- Home health aide - $51,480

---

[34] LongTermCare.gov. February 18, 2020. "How Much Care Will You Need?" https://acl.gov/ltc/basic-needs/how-much-care-will-you-need

[35] Amelia Josephson. smartasset.com. September 2, 2021. "Average Retirement Savings: Are You Normal?" https://smartasset.com/retirement/average-retirement-savings-are-you-normal

- Adult health day care - $16,896
- Assisted living facility - $44,400
- Nursing home (semi-private room) - $104,028

To see the median cost in other states, visit https://www.genworth.com/about-us/industry-expertise/cost-of-care.html.

Long-Term Care Insurance

So why is it that, according to the American Association for Long-Term Care Insurance, only 7.5 million Americans own it? That translates to only a small percentage of American seniors.

Cost is one factor. Let's say a couple, both age fifty-five, want to take out a traditional long-term-care insurance policy that would pay out $164,000 for each of them, and include a 3 percent inflation option. That would cover them for almost two years in a semi-private room in an average Florida nursing home. They would have to pay $3,950 annually for the both of them to be covered.

Traditional long-term-care insurance is like auto insurance. It's a use-or-lose-it proposition. If you pay thousands of dollars into the policy over the years and never need long-term care, that money is down a black hole. Of course, you don't *want* to have to use it.

Also, there is no guarantee your rates will remain the same. An individual who is age sixty, for example, might pay, say, $200 per month for a policy that provides as little as $150 per day for a maximum of three years, then be faced with a rate increase a few years down the road. If they can't afford the rate increase, they are "between a rock and hard place." If they cancel the policy, they lose all they have paid into it.

A New Approach

Insurance companies are in business to make a profit. It has not escaped their notice that that sales of traditional long-term-care insurance aren't exactly soaring. In recent years, they have come up with new and different solutions. One creative approach is to attach long-term-care options to annuities and life insurance policies. These policies are called "combos" by those in the insurance industry, because they combine two coverage elements into one.

There are many variations on this. One is a fixed annuity that provides a guaranteed minimum interest rate with long-term-care features built in, which often involve an additional annual fee. If your funds are ever needed for long-term care, the amount you put in comes out first. Then a benefit is triggered that will, in essence, provide up to two or three times the amount of the annuity for long-term care for a period of time. As an example, if you purchased a $100,000 annuity with a selected benefit limit of 300 percent and a two-year long-term-care benefit factor then you would have an additional $200,000 available for long-term-care expenses, even after the initial $100,000 annuity policy value was depleted. In other words, an annuity purchased with $100,000 could potentially pay out long-term-care benefits of up to $300,000. That is a broad-brush description of the product and provisions, which vary from one insurance company to another. But you get the idea.

Another possible solution for individuals who qualify is life insurance combined with a long-term-care (LTC) rider. These policies are usually purchased with a single premium, just like the annuity. The LTC benefit is usually a small percentage of the death benefit per month.

Let's say someone bought one of these combination life insurance policies and paid a $50,000 premium into a $100,000 life policy with an LTC rider. The cash value (not the surrender value) might be in the neighborhood of $50,000. The LTC benefit would be somewhere around $2,000 per month if long-term care were needed. Whatever money is paid out reduces the policy's cash value by the same amount. In most cases, the applicant must pass a physical to qualify for the insurance, and some policies require financial underwriting as well.

These policies are not for everyone, and there are a few moving parts to them I have not taken the time to detail here. It is best to consult with an insurance professional for a thorough explanation. The point is that traditional LTC insurance is not necessarily the only game in town.

According to the United States Department of Health and Human Services, it's estimated that seven out of ten people who live to the age of sixty-five will need some type of long-term-care services at some point in their lives. Let's say that you were going to fly to a tropical island for a vacation. You get to the airport and you hear an announcement informing you that seven out of ten airplanes are not going to make it to their destinations. Would you even consider getting on board one of those airplanes? I doubt it. Yet, we are essentially taking chances with our fortunes every day by not protecting ourselves in some fashion.

Some people I have discussed this with came into the office under the mistaken impression that Medicare would cover it. Medicare is a wonderful provision for seniors, but it does not pay for long-term care. Medicare Part A (hospital insurance) may cover care given in a certified skilled nursing facility if it's medically necessary, but most nursing home care is custodial care, like help bathing or dressing. Medicare doesn't cover that.

What about Medicaid? You have to be a pauper in the eyes of the government, and a ward of the state to be covered by Medicaid. If you are on Medicaid, your choices are limited as to the quality of your care. Medicaid has gotten very strict about transferring property to qualify for long-term care. They have a five-year look-back period that prevents individuals from giving all of their wealth away to their children just to get Uncle Sam to pick up the tab for the nursing home. They will insist that you "spend down" all of your money, including the value of your home equity. They let you keep $2,000 in the bank for personal items, and they monitor that closely. Typically, they will also let you keep your home.

So, if you don't have insurance, and you aren't covered by Medicare and Medicaid is not an acceptable option, what's left? Your personal assets and those of your family.

There may be no easy or cheap answer to this dilemma, but I advise anyone who values planning over poverty to invest the time to talk to a financial professional and work out a strategy designed to help protect you.

One thing is for certain, if you intend to insure yourself against this possibility (or probability), you need to do so before it happens. Afterward is too late. You can't dial up your insurance company and upgrade your homeowners policy *during* a house fire. Also, your total net worth will determine to some extent the amount of protection you need. It wouldn't make sense to take out a $5 million fire insurance policy on a $1 million home. You need insurance coverage that matches what you stand to lose. The more considerable your assets are, the more you have to protect.

Procrastination is part of human nature. But the longer you wait to buy insurance to protect yourself with long-term care insurance, the costlier it may become. Your health may decline, causing you not to qualify. The older you are, the stricter underwriting is. Also, the older you are, the more expensive it becomes, especially if you go with traditional long-term care.

If you are trying to determine if you need long-term-care insurance of any kind, ask yourself, "How would I pay for assisted living or a nursing home if I needed it right now?" At $400 per day, how long would it take for your personal assets to be depleted?

CHAPTER THIRTEEN

Deciding on Life Insurance? Meet My In-law

I would like to tell you a story about my brother-in-law, David Pavey.

David never had a bad word to say about anyone. He was the type of person who would make friends with strangers in elevators. That's just how he was. David married my sister, Toni. David and Toni had two children, David Blake Pavey and Candance Santina Pavey (now Miller). Both David Blake and Candance Santina are fine young adults now and doing very well for themselves. But let's go back in time to when they were six and three years old, respectively.

Life was good. Toni was a nurse and David a nurse anesthetist. If you know anything about anesthesiology, you know the agents used by these professionals to render the patients unconscious before an operation are gasses. Whenever someone asked David what he did for a living, he would always reply, "I pass gas." It always got a laugh.

I saw how David loved to work hard. And, how he also loved life and spending time with his family. He once mentioned life insurance's purpose during a casual conversation, so I shared observations based on my time in the insurance and financial advisory business. People his age often pass on taking out a life insurance policy because when you're relatively young and healthy, it can be hard for some to justify the need or the expense.

David contemplated the situation for some time until a relatively common health scare convinced him to act. After developing Type 2 diabetes, David got a nice-sized policy, despite his pre-existing condition.

In August 1992, bad news came right around the time Hurricane Andrew barreled toward Florida, leading to massive evacuations. My wife and I were in Maryland when I got the call that David was dying of late-stage lung cancer, an illness doctors had diagnosed about two years after David took out the life insurance policy he took time considering. Six months later, David died with family and friends at his hospital bedside.

My sister was thirty-three at the time, with two young children. The proceeds from the policy enabled Toni to have some help with the children while she worked full time. She was also able to go back to school, get her master's degree, and become a nurse practitioner. Toni eventually remarried and has been blessed with an even larger family now.

The life insurance industry has changed significantly over time. New life insurance contracts are so different that some of them are now considered an asset class.

The New Breed

One financial tool I find intriguing and is available today, that not all advisors know about, is offered by (drum roll, please) insurance companies

Sometimes, when conducting financial seminars, I like to ask the audience, "If you were putting together the perfect financial vehicle, what features would you include?" The responses are interesting. Of course, the *perfect* financial vehicle would have 100 percent liquidity with no risk; provide immediate, double-digit returns; would have no fees; and would have no qualifications. Of course, such a vehicle doesn't exist. There is usually a tradeoff of some kind. For example, a bank CD is safe in that the FDIC insures it, but generally offers low interest rates. A stock market investment has the potential for a double-digit return, but comes with a measure of risk. Let me say for the record, there is no such thing as a perfect financial vehicle. Every product has its trade-offs and restrictions.

But, in a nutshell, here is an overview of some of the features incorporated in index universal life insurance contracts, which offer the following potential benefits:

- Tax deferral – Any cash value built up inside the insurance policy is not taxed, and you can benefit from compounding.
- Tax-free death benefit for heirs (assuming a proper beneficiary designation)
- Not invested in the market
- A level of liquidity for access to a portion of any cash value
- The option to purchase additional home health care benefits

You are probably saying, "Alfie, it sounds too good to be true." Am I right? Where's the catch? Well, there is a catch. It is life insurance, and you must be healthy enough to qualify. This is not to say that you must be a perfect physical specimen. Insurance companies typically understand that many people these days have issues like hypertension (high blood pressure) and diabetes. In many instances they may accept many of these individuals if their conditions are under control. Some even accept cancer survivors if enough time has elapsed between diagnosis and remission. They do, however, tend to charge higher premiums for those with certain medical histories.

Insurance companies regularly revise acceptance standards related to different medical characteristics. For example, the 1980s and '90s, those who tested positive for THC, the primary psychoactive compound in cannabis, typically got declined for insurance. However, tolerance and perception regarding marijuana use has relaxed, especially since many states have legalized marijuana. In accordance with that shifting public sentiment, insurance companies have eased restrictions.[36] We have had clients who tested with THC and received a preferred rating.

Indexed universal life insurance is not a registered security or stock market investment; it doesn't directly participate in any stock or equity investments, or index. At its core, it is still a life insurance policy with the death benefit being its primary benefit. However, it also offers the opportunity to build cash value within the policy by earning interest credits each year that are tied to positive changes in an external market index, such as the S&P 500,

---

[36] Sarah Sharkey. moneyunder30.com. June 18, 2020. "How Does Marijuana Use Affect Your Life Insurance Rates" https://www.moneyunder30.com/how-does-marijuana-use-affect-your-life-insurance-rates

without ever being invested in the market itself. These credits are subject to caps or limits set by the issuing company. The index used is a price index and does not reflect dividends paid on the underlying stocks. Indexed universal life insurance is subject to limitations, including policy fees and charges, as well as health restrictions and, in some cases, financial underwriting. They also involve surrender penalties for withdrawals in the early years of the policy.

You most likely will not divert all of your assets into an IUL policy. At least, I would not advise it. However, if you consider your portfolio to be a large vessel, an IUL policy could be viewed as a dinghy, or lifeboat. The nice feature is the "dinghy," or IUL has the potential to receive competitive growth, and you will owe no taxes. Neither will your heirs owe taxes as beneficiaries of the IUL, if you follow the terms of the policy.[37]

Keeping an Open Mind

As I write this, I am on a plane heading to Dallas, Texas, for some additional training. I do this throughout the year. In addition to the academic training I receive at these functions, it also affords me an opportunity to rub shoulders with my professional peers and learn from them. This enables me to keep up with what is happening in the industry and continue to offer my clients the best retirement planning advice I can.

I keep an open mind at these training events. If you don't keep an open mind, you miss out on opportunities. Methods and

---

[37] Policy loans and withdrawals will reduce available cash values and death benefits and may cause the policy to lapse or affect any guarantees against lapse. Additional premium payments may be required to keep the policy in force. In the event of a lapse, outstanding policy loans in excess of unrecovered cost basis will be subject to ordinary income tax. Tax laws are subject to change. You should consult a tax professional.

strategies that worked well ten years ago may not be as effective today as they once were. A marvelous aspect of a free enterprise society and the free-market system is competition. Insurance companies are in competition with banks and Wall Street for retirees' investment dollars. Their product-design people and actuary teams are constantly at the drawing boards, inventing new ways to help retirees and pre-retirees achieve their goals for independent and secure lifestyles once they quit working. Stubbornly clinging to old ideas or refusing to examine new strategies can be harmful to your wealth.

So, dear reader, all I ask of you is to keep an open mind. See for yourself if these new life insurance products may be something that makes sense as part of your overall financial planning picture. It is human nature to stereotype and shut out new ideas.

My good friend and colleague Sandy Morris held up her cellphone and asked me, "What is this?" I said, "It's an iPhone!" "Really?" she replied. "I use it as a computer, GPS, I check on my accounts; I even use it as a flashlight. Oh yeah, I do make some calls from it when I'm not texting or emailing!"

The point is, even though it's still a phone, its use has changed over time. It is a mini-computer with more data processing capability than the machines that put the first man on the moon. But we still call it a phone, don't we? These new life insurance products are not your grandfather's insurance. We must look at them for what they do, and not what we call them. Like the smartphone, they are tools that serve so many other functions in addition to their original purpose.

CHAPTER FOURTEEN

What's Keeping YOU Up at Night?

During a recent client financial seminar, I asked participants to write down on index cards what was keeping them up at night. When I collected them, the top three answers were:

1. Higher taxes in the future
2. Price hikes caused by inflation
3. The growing national debt

These are, of course, big problems over which the people in the room had no control. But we could, and did, talk about how national and world affairs can affect our financial affairs, and we discussed how we could plan accordingly.

"Who owns most of our country's debt?" I asked the group. The most popular answer to that question is China. But in reality, the biggest holders of U.S. debt are the Social Security trust funds and other federal government accounts, as well as the Federal Reserve banks. Japan actually tops China as the country with the largest foreign holdings of our national debt.[38]

Politics inevitably comes up in these discussions. Which party is better for Wall Street? I tell them that I believe the market is bigger than the presidency.

"Wall Street likes bipartisanship," I said. "It likes checks and balances."

But it is also important to diversify. We talk about how people fall short sometimes by investing too heavily in just one or two asset classes.

Another popular topic is gold, because in temperamental times, when the market goes down, you'll see lots of commercials touting this precious metal as a safe haven – a cure for everything. This causes people to wonder if they should change their financial plan and invest more in gold. But the precious metals market is as subject to speculation and volatility as other markets. At one of our events, we asked, "Gold: what is it good for?" The answer is that gold is good for jewelry.

Inflation is always a topic of concern and in 2020 we began to notice its adverse effect again on consumer prices. Some grocery items rose appreciably, as did gasoline. We rarely see inflation coming. When the economy began reopening in 2021 following coronavirus shutdowns, few anticipated the biggest surge in prices

---

[38] Kimberly Amadeo. thebalance.com. October 8, 2021. "Who Owns the US National Debt?" https://www.thebalance.com/who-owns-the-u-s-national-debt-3306124

in 13 years.[39] People often just don't see inflation coming, even when supply shortages help drive higher prices for goods and services.

Yet if you looked hard enough, it was easy to spot fluctuations with consumer goods. I like to ask, "Have you noticed that cereal boxes are getting smaller?" I've enjoyed Clif Bars for as long as I can remember, and they are definitely getting smaller! Inflation is there, people. It can be hard to see sometimes, especially when core inflation, which excludes oil and gas prices, remains stagnant over a lengthy period. In the U.S., that core marker rose 4.5 percent during a 12-month period ending in June 2021, the largest increase since November 1991.[40].

But inflation is always going to be around and can rise at higher levels in some sectors. Sometimes, higher inflation within a particular industry stems from pressure on supply chains to keep pace with demand. Still, in other sectors, factors such as government policy can trigger higher inflation, such as the 4.69 average inflation rate for medical care between 1935 and 2021.[41] It so happens that medical care is very much an expense that retirees should keep in mind.

When inflation strikes across the board, how do retirees produce income off of their assets during volatile times? During the *accumulation phase* of life, pre-retirees are contributing to their 401(k)s, IRAs and other retirement accounts. Once you

---

[39] Christopher Rugaber. Associated Press. July 13, 2021. "US consumer prices surge in June by the most since 2008" https://apnews.com/article/business-prices-consumer-prices-7c0dceffdbd50a8b1b888af5d3b922ed

[40] Ibid.

[41] In2013dollars.com. 2021. "Medical care priced at $1,000 in 1935 > $51,355.53 in 2021" https://www.in2013dollars.com/Medical-care/price-inflation

retire, you have entered what I like to call the *harvesting phase*. It is when you enter the harvesting phase of your financial life that you really need a financial "navigator" on your side. It is not uncommon these days for people to be retired for almost as long as they worked. So, it's not so much about what you make; it's about how much you will be able to KEEP from what you make. How much you don't LOSE.

Many people are losing some of their hard-earned savings these days in ways they don't even realize. I find that many investors are oblivious to hard-to-find fees in their accounts, and they fail to recognize the potential threat inflation has on their future spending. With the odds in your favor for a long life, it's important to have a financial navigator who can help create an income plan that you won't outlive. These are the kinds of topics we tackle at our monthly financial seminars, quarterly client events and on my weekly "Saving the Investor" radio and TV shows. We work with people through these challenges and strive to help reduce concerns about how world affairs might affect their financial affairs. We may not be able to solve all of the political problems in the world, but we can help prepare listeners, viewers and clients by focusing on what they can do to prepare for them.

What to Expect When You Visit Us

Please allow me to take this opportunity to tell you what to expect when you come to our office in Fort Myers. It was a bank before we bought it and made it our headquarters. We want everyone to feel very comfortable. We truly try to treat our clients as family. They *are* family.

When you decide to put your life's savings with a firm, you must have total confidence in that firm, and the plan of action you agree upon to provide you with comfort and direction for your retirement.

The first appointment is really just getting to know each other. It is also an opportunity for us to know and understand your dreams and goals. We do not want to, nor can we, work with every person who comes into our office. It must be a good fit.

The second appointment is where we take the information we collected during the first appointment and show you what we have found out. This process is very important, because most of the time, you will find out what you actually own, and what you are paying. We reveal any misunderstood or uncommon fees and show you any unnecessary risk we feel you may be taking to obtain the returns on your investments.

In many cases, we are able to help reduce that volatility through diversification. Also, we are usually able to estimate how long your money will last in retirement, and how to make it last throughout your life.

I cannot tell you how many times people come into our office asking me about gold. Or, what if the dollar devalues. Or, what will happen if China goes into recession., or . Or, beginning with the onset of the coronavirus, how the economy would rebound from government-imposed lockdowns on our businesses and schools. We use computer programs the U.S. government used in the 2008 financial crisis to show different scenarios and how your portfolio might perform during times of crisis. They are worth a look-see! We try to look at the total picture and craft for you a sound retirement plan with which you can be comfortable and in which you can have confidence.

By now, you have gathered that I love boating and I really love to take people out and enjoy their company. So before I ever leave the dock, I check the radar, see if any rain is coming and when, and then stay away from pending storms.

The same is true when dealing with the potential of rising taxes. A tax storm could very well be coming that could be tough to avoid, no matter what direction you steer your boat. Government relief stemming from the coronavirus only escalated an alarming debt load the U.S. faces. At some point, the government is going to pay for that debt somehow and every American taxpayer will likely share the burden. The Tax Map we share with our clients at Advantage Retirement Group attempts to mitigate the taxes you will potentially pay and analyzes possibilities for you to rely on tax-free income in retirement.

Imagine relaxing on the deck of the boat with friends or sipping on coffee at a beachfront bistro. Do you want to be the person at the table miffed by how your IRAs are taxed to the hilt, how your tax bracket has changed for the worse, and how your new marginal tax rate affected your Social Security and Medicare? Or, do you want to listen to that rant and be the one who responds, "I don't know what you're talking about? Taxes aren't bothering me."

Again, taxes are one of many retirement topics we address in our Retirement Simulator Process, which attempts to show you the foundation behind a solid retirement and how it should ideally be funded by reliable and predictable income. After determining how much income you will need in retirement, we devise a customized plan for you to follow. To help you enjoy your retirement vision we incorporate a variety of tools into planning for income, investments, taxes, health care, and legacy.

I am not saying that you will not experience volatility, but what I am saying is your plan will be developed to help ensure you are not taking *unnecessary* risk in order to produce returns in your portfolio. Also, it helps ensure you do not go into panic mode like the average investor does when the market enters a downturn.

A good financial navigator helps you take the emotion out of investing by creating a customized retirement income plan. A plan designed to keep you smoothly afloat and avoid choppy waters that could otherwise ensnare you once you enter what I sincerely hope will prove to be the most enjoyable years of your life.

About
the Author

Alfie Tounjian is president and founder of Advantage Retirement Group, a financial advisory firm with offices in Fort Myers and Naples, Florida. The firm's headquarters is in Fort Myers, where Alfie and his wife, Tommie, live and work. Alfie has attained the CERTIFIED FINANCIAL PLANNER™ designation, having become a CFP® professional through American College of Financial Services. He has also earned the Registered Financial Consultant (RFC®) designation and passed the Series 65 securities examination, which makes him a fiduciary. He is also licensed as a life/health/annuity insurance agent.

Alfie shares his financial planning philosophy on his popular radio and television show, "Saving the Investor." He began his career in the financial services profession in 1983 when he relocated to Maryland and opened his first office.

Alfie prefers to liken his help to an experienced navigator rather than managing his clients. He helps them take advantage of proprietary programs and strategies designed to help grow and preserve their financial assets. His techniques are particularly appealing to people who would rather spend time enjoying their lives and retirement, confident in the knowledge that they have a retirement income strategy customized to their needs and goals without their constant attention.

Alfie and his family attend Pastor John and Pam Antonucci's church, The Faith Center, in Fort Myers. He enjoys playing golf on the challenging courses of south Florida and relaxing on his boat when he can on the beautiful waters of the Gulf Coast.

Alfie's Story

Alfie's mother, Sandy Glass, came from a large family. She had two brothers and three sisters, and she was the second youngest of the bunch. She grew up in Henderson, Kentucky. Her father was a hard worker and her mother stayed at home to care of the family.

At the tender age of eleven, Sandy lost her parents. Alfie can only share his mother's memories of his grandparents. His grandfather died of lung disease, and his grandmother from a gall bladder ailment. Following their deaths, his mother moved in with her older sister, Aunt Pat, who had just finished nursing school and now found herself in a position of having to work to take care of her two younger siblings.

From stories he heard, Alfie realized his mom and her younger brother were put in a tough spot at a young age. Between Aunt Pat, Aunt Judy, and Uncle Buddy, they did the best they could to take turns caring for his mom and Uncle Rich."

Alfie's grandmother and grandfather did not have life insurance, which would have helped to affordably raise the young children. This unfortunate oversight motivated Alfie professionally when he became an adult. When his mother was fourteen, she moved from Kentucky and went to live with her brother, Buddy, and his wife in New York. Buddy had a good job, working for IBM.

Alfie remembers his mother incredible beauty and how, during her younger days, she looked much older than her age. Sandy got some modeling jobs in New York, and while she was there, she met Alfie's dad. They married when she was fifteen and moved to California, where his family is from. Alfie's sister, Antoinette Marie (Toni) Tounjian, was brought into the world when my mother was only sixteen. Seventeen months later, Alfie was born.

Alfie really doesn't remember much about his father. He and his mother were divorced when Alfie was five. His father was a Teamster truck driver, which meant he wasn't home very much. Sandy and the children moved to Miami Beach, Florida, in 1966 to be with her older sister, Pat. His mother worked as a waitress, trying to make ends meet. Those years were hard times for the young family.

Early Days with Mother

Alfie occasionally reminisces with his sister about the different apartments we lived in. At times the family lost electricity because his mom didn't have the money to pay the bill. Such hardships, however, forged a tight bond between Toni and Alfie because of the difficulties mother, son, and daughter had to endure. The two kids attended several different schools because the family moved around a lot. At least they got to meet new people each year.

When Alfie was in the fourth grade, his mother had to make the hardest decision of her life – sending him and Toni to Florida Methodist Children's Home.

While that created a difficult time for everyone, Alfie looks back and realizes it was also the right choice. The children's home provided structure for he and his sister. They lived in the same group home with ten other kids, a total of six girls and six boys. Toni was always there to support Alfie. The home had all the kids doing their chores every day. Saturdays, they would get to sleep a little later in the morning. Then on Sunday, there was church service, with a great early dinner afterward.

That year was also prompted a big transition for Alfie and Toni as their father died of lung cancer.

The two siblings flew to California to visit with Dad at his place just before he died. After their father's death, life became more normal because Mom started receiving his Social Security benefit, which helped tremendously in raising Toni and Alfie. The three reunited as a family and moved into a nicer apartment. Sandy moved up the ranks with a major department store. She managed the whole shoe department.

Alfie and Toni always knew their mother loved them more than anything in the world. She taught them the morality of compassion and the value of hard work. Alfie once asked his mother if she wished she had had us later in life and, without hesitation, she said no. Alfie and Toni always knew that what Sandy did was for their protection – to give them something better until she was able to work it out.

Alfie will readily acknowledge that both he and Toni were blessed to have such an amazing, giving, and sharing person in their mother. Alfie will stress that "Mom taught me never to give up, and to have faith to get you through hard times."

He also laughs when relating some of the consequences, especially in the kitchen. Toni often helped with the cooking since their mother worked late hours. One result is that Alfie has not touched a plate of Hamburger Helper since 1976.

Sandy embraces an almost-grown Alfie in 1980 as he prepares for his senior prom.

Teenage Years

Due to Sandy's long hours spent working to provide for her children, Alfie admits he may have had "too much freedom" as he transitioned into adolescence.

"You could say I had too much time on my hands," Alfie recalls. "When I was in seventh grade, we moved from Bradenton to Temple Terrace, Florida. Unfortunately, my first choice of friends was the bad kids in the neighborhood. Needless to say, 'Birds of a feather flock together.' So, I was a handful for my poor mom between the seventh and eighth grades.

"But then something changed my life in 1976 that helped me see things differently. Believe it or not, it was the movie "Rocky," which came out when I was about thirteen or fourteen years old. It just struck a chord so strong with me that it changed me both mentally and physically. I began working out, studying hard, and hanging with a new group of uplifting kids. I have tried to let Sylvester Stallone know how he changed my life, but without success. I will keep trying."

Alfie stands alongside his framed Rocky movie poster in the offices of
Advantage Retirement Group.

Breaking into the business world

One of Alfie's first jobs found him selling shoes at Florsheim Thayer McNeil, an upper-end shoe store in Tampa. Fresh out of high school, the job was great for a kid finding his way in life. One night, an elderly couple came into the shoe store. Okay, they were probably in their mid-sixties, but as a 19-year-old, anyone over forty looked old to Alfie. Their names were Tom and Gerry. That's right, Tom and Gerry.

They started a conversation that turned an ordinary night selling shoes into one of the most memorable exchanges Alfie can recount. The couple posed a question most 19-year-olds never hear. "Every thought about working for yourself?" As a big thinker, even at a young age, Alfie didn't hesitate and told them, "Yes, I have."

The couple didn't disclose the business opportunity they wanted to discuss except that they were in the import-export business. Ever curious, Alfie wanted to know more because that's just who he was and still is, but Tom and Gerry preferred setting up a time to talk. They scheduled an appointment for a week later.

That night over dinner, they began going into different aspects of what they could make available to Alfie before finally disclosing that they were talking about Amway. After Alfie's initial disappointment stemming from the negativity he had heard about the company, Alfie consented to give it a try. He paid around fifty bucks to get started with some products and was introduced to an influential circle of Amway superstars who all seemed to drive Cadillacs or own fancy motorhomes.

The exposure to those higher-ups did not help Alfie succeed in moving up the Amway ladder, but the effort he put in proved instrumental in recognizing what it takes to become an entrepreneur. Event speakers always delivered a positive vibe and stressed an important mantra Alfie has applied ever since: "Work for yourself and hang around with leaders if you want to become one."

Yet, one of the last Amway events he attended had an even greater impact. The three-day gathering in Atlanta concluded with a Sunday church service officiated by a well-known pastor. Alfie had always been a believer in God but had never truly affirmed his commitment. After the sermon, the clergyman told anyone who wanted to accept the Lord as their savior to come forward. Alfie joined in. While standing in line, he felt a sensation rush through his body. Later, he was told it was the Holy Spirit.

"So, although I was not a success in Amway," Alfie says, "Amway was a success with me."

A Career Change for Sandy

Around the time Alfie was picking up invaluable entrepreneurial experience with Amway, Sandy had a career change. She was tired of retail and, in 1981, saw a newspaper advertisement for insurance agents.

At that time, Alfie was in school and working full-time. Yet he understood the magnitude of this opportunity for his mother. He helped her study for her insurance test and rejoiced alongside her when she passed with flying colors. Sandy started her insurance career, by reviewing health insurance, life insurance, and Medicare supplement policies with clients.

Those nights helping his mom study proved advantageous for Alfie. Sandy did so well in her new job that it created an opportunity for Alfie to get into the insurance industry two years later. Shortly after that, Sandy married Alfie's stepfather, Jack Glass.

Alfie said his mother enjoyed helping her clients and was a great listener.

Clients loved Sandy but she had to leave the business because of health reasons. Alfie decided to follow in her footsteps beginning in 1983 when he was just twenty-one. He feared his youthful appearance could hurt his chances, but an industry veteran told him people are more interested in working with people they can relate to and find likable. Then the same insurance professional insisted that Alfie learn his products inside and out. To this day, Alfie prides himself on knowing everything there is to know about what his company offers, whether it involves services, investments, insurance, or legacy planning.

Alfie Tounjian joined by Advisors Excel founders Cody Foster, left, and David Callanan in 2008.

Growing alongside Advisors Excel

For the foreword at the beginning of the book, Cody Foster writes about the remarkable relationship Alfie has developed with Advisors Excel and in particular, Cody and the company's other founder, David Callanan.

As Cody explained, the vision for Advisors Excel was to create an organization that supported the best financial advisors in the country by putting them in a better position to help their clients enjoy retirement.

Some would argue that Alfie would have been smart not to have even listened to the owner of a startup company looking to help grow an established, thriving financial advisory practice like his. Had Alfie not listened, though, he would have made a mistake that many others in the financial industry make by thinking they know everything.

In fact, the personal relationships Cody, David, and the rest of their team wanted to forge would be what would drive Advisors Excel to unforeseen heights.

Their vision? Surround yourself with good, successful people and collaborate with them about ideas and best practices, along with proven concepts, processes, and philosophies...

The secret sauce behind Advisor Excel's emergence as a leader within the financial industry is the people — both those who work for AE and fellow independent advisors from whom Alfie has gained extraordinary insights. Among the ideals Advisors Excel champions is this: *When you work with and learn from the best of the best, you become the best of the best.*

Alfie believes in this principle wholeheartedly and knows how much his friendships and associations helped him when he moved back to his home state of Florida and essentially started his financial advisory practice over from scratch.

Attending events with other advisors from all regions of the country allows Alfie to relate to the tensions involved with running successful businesses. Often, those conversations help to reduce some of the anxieties successful business owners might feel. Whenever any of them speak in front of their peers, they feel comfortable knowing they're among friends.

To this day, Alfie is glad he welcomed Cody into his home to speak to him and other partners about the vision to build Advisors Excel. And yes, everyone fired questions at Cody left and right, but through it all, Alfie marveled at how cool and calm the young entrepreneur was in his own skin. Success enables business owners to trust their instincts. Alfie's decision to believe in young owners of a new financial marketing organization began to forge what has been a rewarding relationship with the people at Advisors Excel.

Life Lessons Learned

Growing up without a lot of money may have been difficult at times, but it taught Alfie a lot about life that he would never have learned otherwise. It gave him the work ethic and strength of character to succeed in the business world.

Meeting new clients from different walks of life is a great satisfaction for Alfie. When he first started in the financial services business in 1983, there was no internet. There were also no twenty-four-hour news channels. Investing was simpler in those days, Alfie remembers.

"These days, it requires much more discipline because we live in an age of information overload," Alfie says. "We are inundated with infomercials, news alerts, phone alerts, and continuous information to make us feel uneasy about the future."

This is why Alfie calls his radio and television show "Saving the Investor."

He makes it his mission to share his knowledge and experience. He does so while spreading a positive message to people, letting them know there are steps they can take and things they can do to grow and safeguard their money, and have the retirement they have always wanted,

What we experience in our early life shapes us later on. When Alfie trained his son and nephew to work alongside him, he insisted that each learn the value of keeping promises. Alfie learned that lesson at a young age and it left a lasting impression.

"Growing up, I was determined to always do anything I told people I was going to do," says Alfie. "When I was nine years old, living with my Aunt Pat, another of my mother's sisters called to talk to Mom. She was out, and so my Aunt Judy asked me what I wanted for Christmas. I told her I wanted a new bicycle. She asked me what kind. I told her a Schwinn Varsity. She asked me what color. I told her green."

"I will get you that bike for Christmas," she promised.

"I was so excited," said Alfie. "I just knew that I would get that bike. Aunt Judy had a heart of gold. She never married and grew up in Kentucky, working in a factory her whole life. She only had a sixth-grade education, but she was a hard worker and did not depend on anyone but herself. Christmas came, but my bike did not. I later found out that my Aunt Judy liked her Busch beer, and probably meant it at the time, but quickly forgot her promise."

Alfie never forgot how disappointing a broken promise can be. To this day, he is careful not to make a promise he cannot keep or say something he cannot do.

"I also learned the hard way the value of planning," said Alfie. "My mother's parents had no plan in place to protect their family when they passed away at a young age. Had they had one, life would have been much better for Mom. As it was, she really never had a childhood."

Alfie says that this is why one of his main concerns in financial planning is the continuation of income for the spouse left behind.

He earnestly dives into what will be the income for a surviving spouse. Then, he sets out to create a plan that addresses as many contingencies as possible.

These are only a few of the experiences that have shaped Alfie, both personally and professionally. Alfie says being a CERTIFIED FINANCIAL PLANNER™ professional is a big responsibility because people who come to his office and decide to do business with him trust him with their life's savings. Instead of presenting cookie-cutter plans and products, Alfie – as a CFP® professional and fiduciary – takes on the responsibility of helping the people who put their trust in him use those life's savings to craft a strategy tailored to their personal goals, dreams, and needs. "That is a responsibility I can never take lightly," Alfie says. "Listening to the retirement wishes of our clients is one of the most important aspects of my job. Being on the receiving end of their birthday wishes flipped the script in a way that provided incredible respect for the relationships I have been fortunate to develop over the years.

"On the day I turned sixty, I enjoyed a long lunch with a friend who just happened to be in on plans many had kept secret. While we dined, our team and many clients filled our office parking lot awaiting my return. Valet parking had been arranged, a giant party tent had been pitched and a DJ played music. I was absolutely shocked and overwhelmed.

"Mary Thompson joined my wife Tommie in orchestrating everything right down to the tiniest of details. Our incredible team helped too in pulling it off. The time spent with all those wonderful people that day convinced me again of just how blessed I am.

"The next day, I spent the morning opening gifts and cards. As I read the messages, tears came to my eyes. I always knew that our company's role was to always look out for our clients and put them in the best position possible. Yet here were our clients, providing me satisfaction in knowing we made such an impact on their lives.

"I am truly humbled to be in this position alongside the best team ever while providing comfort to so many people during their retirement. We have amazing clients, many of whom made my sixtieth a special day I will always remember.

"God is Good!"

Acknowledgments

I want to thank my wife, Tommie, for being my rock and best friend. If it was not for her, I know I would not be where I am today! We are an amazing team! It's been a great forty years together and I'm looking forward to the next chapters.

My son, Devon, makes me proud. He started working for the company in 2021 after graduating from college. It's great to have him as part of the team.

While writing the first book, my mom passed away just before it was finished. I knew she would have been proud because that's who she was, a constant source of inspiration. She was the most loving, caring person I have ever known. Love you to the moon, Mom!

While writing this book, I remember stories from my early years that help shape me. My sister, Toni, has always been there for the family. Life wasn't always easy for us, but we always had each other. My sister takes after our mom and is a very caring person also. She has always looked out for me, even to this day. She has two beautiful children and five grandchildren, who can do no wrong.

Mary Thompson worked very hard with me on this book. I most likely would have put it off for many years if Mary had not been there to push me to dig deeper and keep reminding me that people really do want to know my story. Thank you for all your hard work with this endeavor. What I love about Mary is her love of God and Family.

We continually strive to build Advantage Retirement Group into an independent company featuring a dynamic team rooted in values that help provide the soundest level of retirement planning. We have never pursued a team member through a want-ad. Instead, relationships we first developed outside of work contribute to a warm, caring culture intent on helping you achieve your retirement vision.

We know that financial planning considerations should incorporate the needs and values of entire families. With that in mind, Advantage Retirement Group has assembled a team that will be here for the years ahead, eager and ready to serve our clients for the long term.

Pastor John Antonucci has been not just a great friend, but he has given me the confidence to try things that I never imagined I could do. I now enjoy doing the "Saving the Investor" radio hour of power, and the TV show that has changed me immeasurably. He is also a great, Godly man. And his son David Antonucci is a very important member of our team.

Last but not least, I thank my Lord, Jesus Christ, for giving me this amazing life. My family and I are so grateful for the opportunity to touch the lives of so many people who have become a big part of our lives.

Cheers and Blessings!
~Alfie

The Advantage Retirement Group attending a team retreat at a South Seas resort in 2021: (from left) Colton Bradford, Devon Tounjian, Alfie Tounjian, Tommie Tounjian, Daniella Kowalski, Mary Thompson, and David Antonucci.

Back cover photo: Marty Wisher.

**Official Partner
of FGCU Athletics
2021-2023**

Fort Myers

8870 Daniels Parkway

Fort Myers, FL 33912

Naples

999 Vanderbilt Beach Road

Naples, FL 34108

Phone: 239.561.1155
Fax: 239.288.6206

Email: askalfie@savingtheinvestor.com

Web: advantageretirementgroup.com

Facebook: facebook.com/AdvantageRetirementGroup

LinkedIn: linkedin.com/in/alfie-m-tounjian-cfp ®-rfc-08411426

YouTube: youtube.com/c/Alfie Tounjian/videos

Made in the USA
Middletown, DE
16 April 2023

28921893R00116